HIGHER EDUCATION AND SDG16

"Sarah E. Mendelson and her collaborators make a compelling case for the Sustainable Development Goals (SDGs) as a promising project for re-energizing progress on social justice, economic development, and human rights. In their vision, law remains a guiding standard, but the SDG approach puts law to work with a tool kit of community organization, operational know-how, and rigorously generated data. Academe has a central role to play in educating the new generation of principled pragmatists in the outlook, skills, and information they will need to boost rights and justice to a higher level."

Jack Snyder, Robert and Renée Belfer Professor of International Relations, Political Science Department, Columbia University

"The sobering fact is that the world is falling short of achieving the United Nations' Sustainable Development Goals (SDGs). But the contributors to this volume firmly reject the idea that the goals should be abandoned. Instead of running away from the SDG project, the authors here focus on practical next steps toward global sustainability and human rights. The chapters explore a range of novel ways of localizing the goals. They outline new methods of engaging the next generation of policymakers and scholars in human rights and development work, and highlight important leadership roles that universities can play in effectuating the SDGs going forward. In the process, contributors pinpoint ongoing – but surmountable – barriers to SDG implementation, such as the failure of government entities and researchers to capture disaggregated data that would support successful tailoring of policies to human rights-based goals. This is a book for those who understand that failure is not an option when it comes to the SDGs, and who are ready to lean into a sustainable future through concrete action."

Martha F. Davis, University Distinguished Professor of Law, Northeastern University

Prescient in its exploration of the how inequality has riven United States society and compelling in its urgent call to use the UN Sustainable Development Goals as a framework for doing something about it here and beyond, this book is essential reading for policymakers, academics and advocates alike. Each chapter takes up separate arena for action. All of them center around Goal 16, on the role of higher education in building peace, justice and strong institutions. Each chapter features new primary source data and practical examples of how cities, universities, nongovernmental organizations (NGOs) and social movements together have used the SDGs to build stronger systems of accountability for fulfilling economic rights. The book centers the "unjust recovery" in the wake of the COVID-19 pandemic in order to reveal the deeper systemic flaws that perpetuate inequality, while also making clear that student engagement with the SDGs is key to building the political momentum for tackling it.

Shareen Hertel, Wiktor Osiayński Chair of Human Rights & Political Science, University of Connecticut

HIGHER EDUCATION AND THE SUSTAINABLE DEVELOPMENT GOALS

Series Editor

Wendy Purcell, PhD FRSA
Professor with Rutgers University and Academic Research Scholar with Harvard University; Emeritus Professor and University President Emerita.

About the Series
Higher Education and the Sustainable Development Goals is a series of 17 books that address each of the SDGs in turn specifically through the lens of higher education. Adopting a solutions-based approach, each book focuses on how higher education is advancing delivery of sustainable development and the United Nations Global Goals.

Forthcoming Volumes
Higher Education and SDG10: Reduced Inequalities edited by Priya Grover, Nidhi Phutela, and Pragya Singh

Higher Education and the Sustainable Development Goals

HIGHER EDUCATION AND SDG16

Peace, Justice, and Strong Institutions

EDITED BY

SARAH E. MENDELSON
Carnegie Mellon University, USA

United Kingdom – North America – Japan – India
Malaysia – China

Emerald Publishing Limited
Emerald Publishing, Floor 5, Northspring, 21-23 Wellington Street, Leeds LS1 4DL.

First edition 2025

Editorial matter and selection © 2025 Sarah E. Mendelson.
Individual chapters © 2025 The authors.
Published by Emerald Publishing Limited.

These works are published under the Creative Commons Attribution (CC BY 4.0) licence. Anyone may reproduce, distribute, translate and create derivative works of these works (for both commercial and non-commercial purposes), subject to full attribution to the original publication and authors. The full terms of this licence may be seen at http://creativecommons.org/licences/by/4.0/legalcode.

Reprints and permissions service
Contact: www.copyright.com

No part of this book may be reproduced, stored in a retrieval system, transmitted in any form or by any means electronic, mechanical, photocopying, recording or otherwise without either the prior written permission of the publisher or a licence permitting restricted copying issued in the UK by The Copyright Licensing Agency and in the USA by The Copyright Clearance Center. No responsibility is accepted for the accuracy of information contained in the text, illustrations or advertisements. The opinions expressed in these chapters are not necessarily those of the Author or the publisher.

British Library Cataloguing in Publication Data
A catalogue record for this book is available from the British Library

ISBN: 978-1-80455-895-9 (Print)
ISBN: 978-1-80455-892-8 (Online)
ISBN: 978-1-80455-894-2 (Epub)

INVESTOR IN PEOPLE

In memory of Christof Heyns (1959–2021),
a giant in human rights,
who understood the potential of the
Sustainable Development Goals,
and who left us all far too soon.

CONTENTS

List of Figures and Charts xi
List of Acronyms xiii
Series Editor Preface xv
Acknowledgments xix

1 Introduction: SDG 16, Higher Education, and the Benefits of New Approaches to Teaching and Researching Human Rights
Sarah E. Mendelson 1

2 Closing Access to Justice Gaps Globally
Elizabeth Andersen 13

3 Judicial Institutions, SDGs, and the 2030 Agenda Across Latin America and the Caribbean
Alvaro Herrero 37

4 The Potential of Participatory and Experiential Learning for the Promotion of Human Rights and the SDGs
Thomas Probert 61

5 Toward More Just Societies: The SDG Agenda and Innovations in Higher Education
Ariel C. Armony 79

6 Between Localization and Realization: Partnerships Toward Advancing Human Rights and the Sustainable Development Goals in Los Angeles
Gaea Morales, Anthony Tirado Chase, Michelle E. Anderson and Sofia Gruskin 97

7 Unjust Recovery in the Wake of the Pandemic and the Need to Reframe Human Rights Using the SDGs
  Sarah E. Mendelson   115

About the Editor   145
About the Contributors   147
Index   151

LIST OF FIGURES AND CHARTS

Fig. 6.1	Summary of Task Force Models as Presented by Morales, Chase, and Gruskin at the Carnegie Mellon Workshop on the Margins of the World Justice Forum 2022.	105
Fig. 6.2	Maternal Mortality Ratio Data from L.A. SDGs Data Reporting Platform.	110
Chart 7.1	Households on SNAP in Pittsburgh by Race, 2015–2021.	132
Chart 7.2	Households on SNAP in Atlanta by Race, 2015–2021.	132
Chart 7.3	Unemployment Rate in Pittsburgh by Race, 2015–2021.	134
Chart 7.4	Unemployment Rate in Atlanta by Race, 2015–2021.	135
Chart 7.5	United States Maternal Mortality Rate by Race, 2018–2021.	135

LIST OF ACRONYMS

ARPA	American Rescue Plan Act
CDC	Centers for Disease Control and Prevention
CHANGE	City Hub and Network for Gender Equity
CMU	Carnegie Mellon University
GAO	Government Accountability Office
HEI	Higher Education Institutions
HLPF	High-Level Political Forum
HRC	Human Rights Council
ICESCR	International Covenant on Economic, Social and Cultural Rights
IRB	Institutional Review Board
JR	Just Recovery
L.A.	Los Angeles
L.A. SDGs	Los Angeles Sustainable Development Goals
L.A. TFs	Los Angeles Task Forces
LNOB	Leave No One Behind
MDGs	Millennium Development Goals
MMRCs	Maternal Mortality Review Committees
MOIA	Mayor's Office of International Affairs
NGOs	Nongovernmental Organizations
SDGs	Sustainable Development Goals
SNAP	Supplemental Nutrition Assistance Program
TF	Task Force
THE-IR	Times Higher Education Impact Ranking
UDHR	Universal Declaration of Human Rights
UN	United Nations
UNDP	United Nations Development Programme

UNESCO	United Nations Educational, Scientific and Cultural Organization
UNODC	United Nations Office on Drugs and Crime
US	United States
USAID	United States Agency for International Development
VLRs	Voluntary Local Reviews
VNRs	Voluntary National Reviews
VUR	Voluntary University Reviews
WJP	World Justice Project

SERIES EDITOR PREFACE
Professor Wendy Purcell, PhD FRSA

Higher education (HE) makes an important contribution to realizing the Sustainable Development Goals (SDGs). Teaching and learning support the development of responsible citizens as scholars, leaders, entrepreneurs, and professionals. Curiosity-driven and socially impactful research and innovation help advance knowledge frontiers and find solutions for the world's most pressing issues. As anchor institutions, universities and colleges are also active in civic and community settings, working in partnership with other stakeholders. Given the fierce urgency of (un)sustainable development, the climate crisis, and widening inequity within countries and across the globe, HE institutions (HEIs) need to do more and go faster to deliver fully on their potential to help achieve the SDGs.

The book series addresses the role of HE in advancing the SDGs, identifying some actionable and scalable initiatives, and pointing to opportunities ahead. In sharing the ways and means universities and colleges across the world are engaging with the SDGs, the series seeks to both inspire and enable those in the HE sector and stakeholders beyond to transform what they do and how they do it and thereby hasten progress toward Agenda 2030. Insights gleaned from case studies, reflective accounts, and student stories can help the HE sector both deepen and accelerate its engagement with the SDGs. Each book seeks to capture examples of how HEIs are fulfilling the delivery of their academic mission *and* progressing the SDG concerned. Illustrating the work of students, faculty, and staff of the institution, and that undertaken in collaboration with others, positions HE as a change agent operating at a systems level to help create a world that leaves no one behind.

This volume focuses on HE and SDG16 "Peace, Justice, and Strong Institutions" and highlights the work of universities and colleges in achieving this goal to "Promote peaceful and inclusive societies for sustainable development, provide access to justice for all, and build effective, accountable, and inclusive institutions at all levels." SDG16 is intimately entwined with all the other SDGs and is a key determinant in their delivery, advancing equity, and enabling solutions in pursuit of sustainability – transforming our world so that the human rights of all can be realized. Some five billion people however are estimated to have unmet justice needs, ranging from concerns over legal identity, to property rights and access to justice, and this demands a paradigm shift in how to consider human rights using the SDGs.

Curated cases and examples from across the globe are explored to illustrate how progress toward SDG16 is being made through the academic activities of HEIs as well as their work in partnership with other organizations and groups. Everyone should be able to live in peace, feel safe, and be free of the threat of violence whether physical or psychological with explicit protection for vulnerable populations. Working with justice sector institutions, HEIs can support access to justice services as well as help citizens participate in associated governance matters. These networks can be leveraged for student learning opportunities as well offering a source for research questions. This academic engagement can enable the co-creation of solutions with the community that support human rights and tackle abuses and barriers to drive radical inclusion and help improve the lives of everyone in an effort to leave no one behind.

While the SDGs represent global goals, the local dimension is what counts in terms of people's lived experiences. So too then HEIs need to act locally and connect globally. This book calls out the importance of adopting a data-centric approach, with data gaps and data holes filled by university research, innovation, and outreach efforts. In this way, the actuality of people's justice needs is better understood and can help shape the systematic transformation of justice services and institutions. Universities and colleges will also educate and train new cadres of scholars and practitioners who are genuinely empathic to people's justice needs, with experience of justice in action, and focused on strengthening the justice system as a matter of collective urgency.

Universities and colleges play a critical role in developing new systemic and transformative solutions through interdisciplinary and multi-stakeholder collaboration and a purposeful focus on the SDGs. As organizations that have stood for many centuries in some cases, this demands that they adapt to new models of learning, research partnerships, and leadership and governance frameworks. Immersive engagement with the SDGs can catalyze pedagogic innovation, serve to refresh curricula, and stimulate new program development. It can also open new avenues for research, attract new sources of funding, and energize people to deliver on the academic mission. SDG16 is an enabler of sustainable development and vital to the pursuit of sustainability and the health of people, planet, and shared prosperity. This book illustrates this approach with HEIs bringing their key assets of curiosity and the pursuit of knowledge and its application to partners seeking solutions and driving innovation, operating in both local and global networks. Sustainability is a goal for today, and sustainable development is an organizing principle for universities and colleges.

ACKNOWLEDGMENTS

I would like to thank all the contributors to this edited volume and Wendy Purcell for inviting me to take on this opportunity and use this platform to express views that have been percolating for some time. The team at Emerald Publishing has been endlessly patient as we encountered various hurdles. I thank all the CMU students who participated in the Heinz capstone, Krista Rasmussen for her insights, and Sofia Gruskin who met separately with our students and generously shared the L.A. experience. Daniel Armanios and Adam Kolig helped get some charts over the finish line. I thank The Rockefeller Foundation and the David and Lucile Packard Foundation for generous support, and specifically, Nathalia A.M. dos Santos, Zia Khan, and Nancy Lindborg, as well as the Bellagio Center team for graciously hosting our community of practice, the participants of which I also thank for their partnership. Susan Reichle and Ashok Regmi were early supporters and co-conspirators. Tony Pipa, John McArthur, and the Brookings Institution's Center for Sustainable Development as well as the 17 Rooms team have all offered so much intellectual companionship on the SDGs. I thank the participants of the Room 16 discussions in 2020 and 2021 (and my co-moderators Nancy Lindborg and Betsy Andersen) who contributed to the shaping of this book. We mourn the loss of the great Christof Heyns who would, no doubt, have joined Thomas Probert as a co-author. Christof's intellectual contributions, nevertheless, are woven throughout this volume in various ways. Jack Snyder always deserves my thanks for being willing to read my work for literally decades. Many thanks to Michael Yonas and to two anonymous reviewers for their timely and careful reading of chapters. I thank Robin Cole for endless retrievals of articles and helping organize meetings, and Keith Webster for helping make this edited volume an open-source publication (among his many other forms of support of this work). Krishnan, the members of the Heinz Senior Management Team (2018-2024), and Marie Coleman deserve thanks for good naturedly withstanding my SDG obsession, and my colleagues on the CMU Sustainability Initiative as well as Jim Garrett for sharing it. Most of all, thanks to John Harvey, for everything, and for every day we had.

Sarah E. Mendelson

1

INTRODUCTION: SDG 16, HIGHER EDUCATION, AND THE BENEFITS OF NEW APPROACHES TO TEACHING AND RESEARCHING HUMAN RIGHTS

Sarah E. Mendelson

Carnegie Mellon University, USA

ABSTRACT

Why and how should scholars, students, and practitioners engage the Sustainable Development Goals (SDGs) to help reframe and refresh how human rights is taught, understood, and lived? This chapter, and indeed all the chapters in this edited volume, answer this question from a variety of perspectives. Binding them together is the belief that business as usual is not working; while international and national legal frameworks are necessary, they are not sufficient for delivering justice, particularly when it comes to addressing socioeconomic gaps. Getting all this right is more than an academic or UN-driven exercise. Closing these gaps is essential to democracies delivering and requires paradigm shifts. In an era of doom and gloom, the good news is that innovations in higher education, another binding theme, can help grow the next generation that will deliver human rights and sustainable development well beyond 2030.

Keywords: Sustainable Development Goals; human rights; data; democracy delivering; paradigm shift; experiential learning

Why would or should the Sustainable Development Goals (SDGs), and SDG 16 in particular ("peace, justice, and strong institutions") be of interest to scholars researching human rights, to professors engaging students on human rights, to students who are beginning their careers hoping to advance human rights, and indeed, to practitioners working to make human rights real?[1] In short, because of both the universality and the intersectionality of the SDGs, and how they represent a 21st century way of understanding the range of rights encompassed in the Universal Declaration of Human Rights (UDHR).[2] Rights cannot be separated from development, and development cannot be siloed from peace.

In 2015, the global community adopted the 2030 Agenda and the SDGs with the principle of "leave no one behind."[3] This framework is scheduled to run through 2030. The relevance of the framework, however, will likely extend for decades to come. Moreover, the SDGs were presciently built to address the challenges that have emerged as urgent in many communities – from inequality to the climate crisis, from pandemics to declines in life expectancy, from an increase in violence and conflict to the enabling of corruption. It is a framework that recognizes development happens

---

[1] United Nations General Assembly, "Transforming Our World: the 2030 Agenda for Sustainable Development," A/Res/70/1, September 25, 2015, https://www.unfpa.org/sites/default/files/resource-pdf/Resolution_A_RES_70_1_EN.pdf.

[2] On the UDHR, see https://www.un.org/en/about-us/universal-declaration-of-human-rights.

[3] "Transforming Our World: the 2030 Agenda for Sustainable Development," Resolution adopted by General Assembly on September 25, 2015, A/Res/70/1, https://www.un.org/en/development/desa/population/migration/generalassembly/docs/globalcompact/A_RES_70_1_E.pdf.

everywhere – not just in the "global south" or in so-called "developing" countries.

Awash in crises at the midpoint of the world's commitment to the 2030 Agenda, there are numerous calls to "rescue" the SDGs, most prominently from the United Nations (UN) Secretary-General.[4] Meanwhile, in the human rights community, a downbeat cottage industry has arisen (again) around pessimistic themes such as the "end times" and a failed, "last utopia."[5]

This volume details multiple pathways out of such doom and gloom and helps advance the closely aligned and timely endeavors of creating peaceful, just, and inclusive communities – exactly what SDG 16 is all about. The volume explores ways in which innovations in higher education, and specifically, how human rights and the SDGs are taught, can help make relevant human rights in the 21st century for new generations. Universities have a critical role to play in creating SDG literacy as well as a refreshed approach to human rights education, or a paradigm shift, helping to grow what I have called "Cohort 2030."[6]

---

[4] "Rescuing the SDGs: General Assembly Highlights 'World's to do List,'" *UN News*, September 19, 2022, https://news.un.org/en/story/2022/09/1126981.

[5] Stephen Hopgood, *The Endtimes of Human Rights* (Cornell University Press, 2013); Samuel Moyn, *The Last Utopia: Human Rights in History* (Belnap Press, 2012). Lamenting specific aspects of human rights, including a decrease in effectiveness, is not unique to the last decade. See David Rieff, "The Precarious Triumph of Human Rights," *New York Times*, August 8, 1999, https://www.nytimes.com/1999/08/08/magazine/the-precarious-triumph-of-human-rights.html and Sarah E. Mendelson, "Dusk or Dawn for the Human Rights Movement?," *The Washington Quarterly* 32, no. 2 (2009, April): 103–20. https://ciaotest.cc.columbia.edu/journals/twq/v32i2/f_0016183_13957.pdf. It's also worth noting that some scholars worry specifically about the harm caused by negative framing around human rights. See Kathryn Sikkink, "A Cautionary Note about the Frame of Peril and Crisis in Human Rights Activism," in *Rising to the Populist Challenge: A New Playbook for Human Rights Actors*, ed. César Rodríguez-Garavito and Krizna Gomez (Dejusticia, 2018), 171–82, https://dash.harvard.edu/bitstream/handle/1/37143007/rising-to-the-populist-challenge-version-final-para-web-1.pdf?sequence=6&isAllowed=y.

[6] Sarah Mendelson, "Young People, the Sustainable Development Goals, and the Liberal World Order: What is to be done?" *Medium*,

In this introduction, I reflect briefly on why such a paradigm shift is needed. John W. McArthur, the Brookings Institution scholar, reminds us that "doing things differently is central to the purpose of the SDGs." Quoting the 2030 agenda, he notes that the SDGs are about "'transforming our world,'" and the "'universal, integrated, and interrelated nature'" of the SDGs "'seek(s) to realize the human rights of all.'"[7] While those statements may be commonplace to some readers, many in the human rights community know nothing about the SDGs or may feel that because they are voluntary and not legally binding, they are not relevant. There is, however, something of a counter movement developing, including and going beyond senior scholars and practitioners from the human rights community represented in this volume.[8] There is a growing sense that the emphasis on legal frameworks has been too abstract and that the type of rights most associated with the human rights movement, namely political ones, has been too narrow, too predictable, and often disconnected from the pressing, unmet needs of local populations.

The UDHR continues to be *the* framing document on rights relevant for the 21st century. But many aspects of it have been unevenly adopted. The United States, despite its role as a global leader on human rights, has downplayed the socioeconomic elements of the UDHR for decades. This oversight – intentional during the Cold War, and largely unchallenged in the post-Cold War triumphalist period – helped contribute to the extreme inequalities and inequities plaguing the country 25 years into the 21st century. The United

---

October 9, 2018, https://medium.com/sdg16plus/young-people-the-sustainable-development-goals-and-the-liberal-world-order-what-is-to-be-done-fc648e3b2d21.

[7] John W. McArthur, "The 'Second Half' of the Sustainable Development Goal era: Ideas for doing things differently," *The Brookings Institution*, April 5, 2023. https://www.brookings.edu/articles/the-second-half-of-the-sustainable-development-goal-era-ideas-for-doing-things-differently/.

[8] César Rodríguez-Garavito, "Human Rights 2030: Existential Challenges and a New Paradigm for the Field" (Public Law and Legal Theory Research Paper Series, Working Paper No. 21-39, June 2021). https://static1.squarespace.com/static/648b6a7183cd201b2ba91d28/t/648c6f4b95e1153483c682e0/1686925141063/Human+Rights+2030.pdf.

States is not the only democracy failing to deliver for large swathes of its populations; authoritarian forces are taking advantage of that fact. At the same time, the downbeat and pessimistic academic cottage industry concerning human rights has developed precisely because the legal frameworks are so often ignored. Thus, the doom and gloom loop.

Another factor driving the need for new approaches to human rights relates to what might be understood as "the health of civil society." As a Russia scholar, starting over 20 years ago in the early 2000s, I was exposed to gross human rights violations, the phenomenon of closing space and other threats to civil society – all signs to come of the ever more catastrophic trouble wrought by the Putin regime. I was, however, also aware that many in the Russian human rights community had little interest in engaging the larger public – a condition that would surely contribute to their societal and political isolation. The activists were more closely aligned with donors in New York and Geneva than their neighbors in Moscow, Perm, or Ryazan.[9] That struck me then as a serious problem. Fast forward 20 years later, most members of the Russian human rights movement have either been murdered, jailed, or live in exile.

The health of civil society would only get worse and not just for Russian human rights activists. By the time I was serving in the Obama administration, between 2010 and 2017, what was known as "the closing space phenomenon" around the world would evolve into its own epidemic.[10] In many places, nongovernmental organizations (NGOs) were portrayed as "alien" or "foreign agents." Governments would share laws country-to-country and then adopt

---

[9] Sarah E. Mendelson and Theodore P. Gerber, "Activist Culture and Transnational Diffusion: Social Marketing and Human Rights Groups in Russia," *Post-Soviet Affairs* 23, no. 1 (2007): 50–75, http://investigadores.cide.edu/crow/wp-content/uploads/2015/11/Mendelson-Gerber-2007-Activist-Culture-and-Transnational-Diffusion-Social-Marketing-and-Human-Rights-Groups-in-Russia.pdf.

[10] Sarah E. Mendelson, "Why Governments Target Civil Society and What Can Be Done: A New Agenda," *CSIS*, April 2015, http://investigadores.cide.edu/crow/wp-content/uploads/2015/11/Mendelson-Gerber-2007-Activist-Culture-and-Transnational-Diffusion-Social-Marketing-and-Human-Rights-Groups-in-Russia.pdf.

draconian versions in their own country not unlike the Russian ones – which have been on overdrive with 50 new, repressive laws passed between 2018 and 2023.[11] The murder of Russian political activist Alexei Navalny in February 2024 shocked most but did not surprise many given the long list of those the Kremlin considered enemies and who have since perished.[12] In country after country, the public and policy responses to such violence have largely been full of sentiment but not much else. More signs of trouble concerning the health of global civil society.

While the closing space phenomenon was gaining speed, however, between 2012 and 2015, the SDGs were also coming together. From my perch at USAID, leading the agency's democracy, human rights, and governance work (and, in the US interagency process for what eventually became SDG 16), that emerging framework held the promise of stimulating a possible refresh, or renewal, with the potential to help deliver rights – a way to drive outcomes, results, and relevance. The SDG framework recognized that development happens everywhere and revealed the interconnectedness of so many issues that had previously been siloed, including rights and development. It could enable tackling problems domestically in the United States that by the 2020s were clearly seen as relevant to the global human rights movement, such as deep and sustained inequalities. Addressing them would also be important for credibility in US foreign policy advancing human rights and democracy around the world. Specifically, the SDGs elevated socioeconomic issues which, from an American perspective, had been set aside or siloed in favor of issues relating to political rights – by not just the US government but many in civil society.[13]

---

[11] International Federation for Human Rights, "The Last 50: Russian Repressive Laws Since 2018," *Mediazona*, June 8, 2023, https://en.zona.media/article/2023/06/07/50rep_en.

[12] Alexey Gusev, "Navalny's Death Highlights a New, Global Division on Political Violence," *Carnegie Endowment for International Peace*, February 21, 2024, https://carnegieendowment.org/politika/91699.

[13] Sarah E. Mendelson, "Inequality, the SDGs, and the Human Rights Movement in the US and Around the World," *The Brookings Institution*, June 12, 2020, https://www.brookings.edu/articles/inequality-the-sdgs-and-the-human-rights-movement-in-the-us-and-around-the-world/.

The bill for that bargain in the United States came due in 2020. The COVID-19 pandemic powered multiple dynamics including a long over-due reorientation. The previously prioritized gaze to abuses abroad rather than across town became untenable for many of us who had worked internationally all our lives. The vast inequalities in the United States emerged as both development and human rights issues. The SDGs seemed even more relevant, not less.[14]

With the adoption of the SDGs, I was not alone in viewing a 21st-century way of understanding the range of rights encompassed in the UDHR. Most recently, that understanding has been boosted by none other than the UN's Office of the High Commissioner for Human Rights. The High Commissioner, Volker Türk, notes that the SDGs come from the human rights treaty bodies and mechanisms that have existed for 75 years. Speaking in April 2023 in Washington at CSIS, he argued "95% of SDGs are anchored in human rights obligations."[15]

Fundamentally, what is relevant about the SDGs for the health of civil society and other communities, shared by those in this volume and others who joined us in May 2023 for a strategic convening at The Rockefeller Foundation's Bellagio Center, is taking the concept of "leave no one behind" seriously, and then using data – especially disaggregated data by gender, race, class, locality – to help shape demand-driven policy responses to the social justice gaps that, in fact, have left many behind. Compared with traditional approaches to human rights, this method is different from an exclusive focus on treaties or conventions that states have or have not signed on to.

---

[14] Sarah E. Mendelson, "The US Is Leaving Millions Behind: American Exceptionalism Needs to Change by 2030," *The Brookings Institutions*, April 10, 2023, https://www.brookings.edu/articles/the-us-is-leaving-millions-behind-american-exceptionalism-needs-to-change-by-2030/.

[15] "The UDHR at 75: A Conversation with UN High Commissioner for Human Rights Volker Türk," *CSIS Human Rights Initiative*, April 18, 2023, https://www.csis.org/events/udhr-75-conversation-un-high-commissioner-human-rights-volker-turk. See also "The Human Rights Guide to the Sustainable Development Goals," *The Danish Institute for Human Rights Methodology*, https://sdg.humanrights.dk/sites/sdg.humanrights.dk/files/SDG%20database%20methodology_0.pdf.

This approach does not negate the importance of legal frameworks. It is rather to suggest an additional approach is needed, particularly when researching and engaging students as well as local communities: growing a Community of Practice – including the authors in this edited volume and going well beyond, to include those who are engaged in field building using the SDGs to improve the quality of people's lives – to refresh and renew how we think of and measure human rights using disaggregated data.

Creating a discipline that listens and responds to people's justice needs is one important aspect of democratic renewal described in several chapters in this book. Such a discipline should not be understood as merely academic. To quote Claudia López, the then-mayor of Bogotá, Colombia, speaking in April 2023 at the "Cities Summit of the Americas" in Denver,

> *The future of humanity lives in cities. How do we build the cities according to the SDGs… [to meet] the social justice challenges? Colombia won't meet the SDGs without cities…take care of people first if we want them [people] to take care of democracy…dictators who don't care about their own people don't care about the planet.*[16]

At this midway point to 2030, we need to work differently and field build sustainable development.[17] While several chapters in this volume explicitly address access to justice (SDG 16.3), the focus in other chapters goes beyond SDG 16 to enliven what is referred to as the SDG16+ agenda for peaceful, just and inclusive communities.[18] Multiple SDGs – including SDG 1 (no poverty), SDG 2 (zero hunger), SDG 3 (good health and well-being), SDG 4 (quality education), SDG 5 (gender equality), SDG 10 (reduced inequalities), SDG 11 (sustainable cities and communities), and SDG 17

---

[16] https://www.citiessummitoftheamericas.org/agenda.
[17] Sarah E. Mendelson, "Building the Field of Sustainable Development," *Stanford Social Innovation Review*, Winter 2020, https://ssir.org/articles/entry/foundations_should_invest_in_building_the_field_of_sustainable_development.
[18] https://cic.nyu.edu/program/pathfinders-for-peaceful-just-and-inclusive-societies/.

(partnerships for the goals) – are touched on in various ways in several chapters.

This volume, like most, is a product of its time. It emerged from Zoom discussions held in the summers of 2020 and 2021 as part of the Brookings Institution and The Rockefeller Foundation flagship "17 Rooms" exercise with several of the authors joining me (and Nancy Lindborg in 2020 as co-moderator, and Elizabeth Andersen in 2021 as co-moderator).[19] This volume also benefited from discussion at the Bellagio Center in May 2023 as well as an earlier related event in July 2019. I thank the participants in all of these convenings for sharing their insights.

In summer 2020, as communities around the world hunkered down in isolation due to COVID-19, and as the United States underwent a (partial) social justice awakening, in Room 16 (of 17), we posited that there might be a real break with the past – and the opportunity for a "just recovery" going forward.[20] With trillions of dollars being spent around the world, we thought the moment for a reset was possible; whatever pressing social justice gaps that preceded the pandemic might successfully be closed. In summer 2021, we continued with that line of inquiry although by then, we had some data to suggest that the hoped for "just recovery" had not and would not come to pass.[21] The issues that were laid bare by the pandemic, however, necessitated thinking differently concerning what we understood to be pressing human rights issues as well as the delivery of human rights, one refreshed by association with the framework of the SDGs.

The authors of these chapters have deep experience in human rights and are engaging the SDGs to help refresh approaches to human rights. In Chapter 2, Elizabeth Andersen discusses the contributions that higher education can make to help the 5.1 billion people globally who have unmet justice needs. Closing the

---

[19] https://www.brookings.edu/projects/17-rooms/.
[20] Nancy Lindborg and Sarah Mendelson, *Room 16*, November 2020, https://www.brookings.edu/wp-content/uploads/2020/11/16.pdf.
[21] Elizabeth Andersen and Sarah Mendelson, *Room 16*, November 2021, https://www.brookings.edu/wp-content/uploads/2021/11/2021-Room-documents_Room16.pdf.

massive justice gap requires new ways of thinking about justice services, and universities can play a significant role by bringing contemporary data analytics, multi-disciplinary collaboration, and innovation to bear in advancing a new people-centered approach to delivering "equal access to justice for all." Alvaro Herrero's Chapter 3 analyzes the nexus between the judiciary and the SDGs, with a particular focus on the experiences of justice sector institutions in localizing SDG 16. In general, judiciaries have been reluctant, or at least passive, in taking responsibility for measuring and implementing the goals of the 2030 Agenda. Herrero makes specific recommendations on how higher education can help shift the culture that permeates justice sector institutions in Latin America and the Caribbean. Thomas Probert's Chapter 4 is especially poignant as he reflects on the power of the work that his mentor and our friend Christof Heyns, a giant in the field of international human rights law and to whom this volume is dedicated, did as he pioneered merging moot courts and the SDGs. Thomas begins by highlighting the significance of human rights education as part of a broader SDG16+ agenda, and on two methods developed in the sphere of human rights education – moot courts and shadow reporting – and contemplates the broader application of these participatory techniques as vehicles to activate the next generation as champions of sustainable development. He proposes means for research and advocacy around topics of interest and concern to students in their local context and argues that an appropriate introduction to the mechanics of development work, at both national and international levels, can excite and inspire engagement with Agenda 2030. In Chapter 5, Ariel Armony explores three questions relating to the SDGs and Higher Education: How can we incorporate the SDG agenda across the Higher Education curriculum? Are SDGs a marketing strategy for universities? How can the SDG agenda help improve collaborations between Higher Education institutions in the global south and global north? Gaea Morales, Anthony Chase, Michelle E. Anderson, and Sofia Gruskin in Chapter 6 explore what the SDGs and human rights look like in practice at the local level drawing on a partnership between local universities and the office of the mayor of Los Angeles. The co-creation of student "Task Forces" with city officials and the use of the SDGs in planning over time showed how localization created opportunities to identify and act on human rights issues through SDG implementation at the city level. In Chapter 7, with contributions from CMU students, I report on an effort to assess the impact of COVID-19 relief funds in two American cities and find social justice needs unmet. Like my colleagues in this volume, most of my professional life has been focused on international human rights and development. The dramatic inequities that the pandemic laid bare led many of us to assess disparities closer to home. The research grounds my argument for a paradigm shift in how we teach and train human rights using the SDGs.

Uptake of the SDGs by those researching and teaching human rights is in no way guaranteed. A large share of the global human rights community does not embrace – let alone know about – the SDGs. Ambivalence in this community is driven (again) in part by the voluntary nature of the SDG agenda, as opposed to one shaped by legal obligations. (Although, as one State Department lawyer pointed out to me, almost all of what the UN does is not legally binding.) The authors of this volume and I, however, hope that our chapters will collectively tackle some of that ambivalence. A new approach that goes beyond laws does require a paradigm shift in the methods that currently dominate human rights education. We are proposing that this takes place through partnership with a Community of Practice – a network of experts using new models and generating innovative learning agendas together with local stakeholders. If you, reader, are interested in such a community, we invite you to engage with us.

This volume has obvious limitations. Our chapters do not cover the world. There is much more to be written about concerning the intersection of human rights and the SDGs plus the numerous challenges confronting the globe. We hope that this volume, however, will stimulate additional research and help show younger as well as older generations how the SDGs are relevant to addressing these and many other challenges that have yet to be solved.

2

CLOSING ACCESS TO JUSTICE GAPS GLOBALLY

Elizabeth Andersen

World Justice Project, USA

ABSTRACT

Over halfway through the implementation of the Sustainable Development Goals, SDG16's promise of access to justice for all remains a distant pipe-dream. Progress has been limited as the COVID-19 pandemic, new armed conflicts, and rising authoritarianism have in many jurisdictions exacerbated justice problems and hobbled institutional responses. Reversing these negative trends and closing the justice gap will require new ways of conceptualizing and delivering justice services, taking a people-centered, problem-solving approach that draws on data about people's justice needs and marshals multi-disciplinary expertise, cross-sectoral collaboration, and innovative policy tools to solve them. Drawing on the analysis of an unprecedented global legal needs survey covering over 100 countries, this chapter describes this challenge and highlights the critical role that institutions of higher education can play in stimulating and supporting the much-needed transformation of our justice systems. It profiles exemplary initiatives at colleges and universities bringing their capabilities to bear on the justice challenge and draws lessons learned for institutions looking to follow suit. In doing so, institutions of higher education can not only help close the justice gap but also build trust in justice institutions and contribute to a rejuvenation of the human rights movement.

Keywords: Access to justice; people-centered justice; legal needs; data; innovation; multi-disciplinary

INTRODUCTION

Sustainable Development Goal 16 (SDG16) promises access to justice for all, underscoring the importance of effective, accessible justice systems for sustainable development. Unfortunately, halfway through the 15-year SDG process, realizing this goal remains illusory. Research suggests that as many as 5.1 billion people have unmet justice needs.[1] This global justice gap includes 1.1 billion people who lack legal identity, 2.1 billion who work in the informal economy, 2.3 billion who lack proof of land tenure or housing rights, and 1.4 billion who lack access to justice to solve their everyday civil justice problems.[2] Many of these deprivations are overlapping and cascading in people's lives, disproportionately affecting poor and marginalized populations and significantly confounding efforts to "leave no one behind."[3]

Closing this massive justice gap requires new ways of thinking about justice services and how societies deliver them. An emerging new people-centered approach to justice draws on contemporary data analytics to improve understanding of people's justice needs

---

[1] "Measuring the Justice Gap: A People-Centered Assessment of Unmet Justice Needs Around the World," The World Justice Project, June 2019, https://worldjusticeproject.org/our-work/research-and-data/access-justice/measuring-justice-gap.
[2] The World Justice Project, "Measuring the Justice Gap."
[3] "Leaving No One Behind: Equality and Non-discrimination at the Heart of Sustainable Development," United Nations, 2017, https://unsceb.org/sites/default/files/imported_files/CEB%20equality%20framework-A4-web-rev3.pdf.

and transform justice institutions to meet those needs. A robust justice data ecosystem coupled with multi-stakeholder collaboration and innovation can help meaningfully improve access to justice. As multi-disciplinary centers of innovation and excellence, universities have a particularly significant role to play in bringing these methodologies to bear.

This chapter will highlight ways in which colleges and universities can help with this justice system transformation, profile exemplary efforts to harness the capacities of higher education in this effort, and identify lessons learned. Universities can make important contributions to developing an effective justice data ecosystem and promoting cross-sectoral collaboration and innovation to meet people's justice needs. Such leadership in higher education promises to help close the justice gap while developing new tools and approaches to advancing human rights and seeding a much-needed rejuvenation of the human rights movement.

GRASPING THE JUSTICE GAP: DATA, INNOVATION, AND COLLABORATION

Making progress toward SDG16's goal of "access to justice for all" requires a radical rethinking of justice sector policies and services, taking as a point of departure the needs and experiences of people whom justice systems are intended to serve. Data is critical to this people-centered approach, to understand people's needs and experiences of the justice system. The data tell a sobering story: our justice systems and current approaches to justice sector policy making and development are failing. Armed with these data insights, policy makers must employ outside-the-box thinking to identify innovative new ways of meeting people's justice needs, including the use of non-legal tools and services, preventive approaches, and collaboration across sectors. Unfortunately, justice systems seriously lag other sectors in their capacity to gather and analyze data across relevant institutions, and they are often resistant to innovation and insulated from other sectors that are critical to finding sustainable solutions to justice problems. Breaking down these barriers to a data-driven, evidence-based, innovative, and collaborative approach to delivering justice is essential to closing the global justice gap.

Taking a People-Centered Approach

In most jurisdictions, justice sector policy making is done by and for justice institutions and actors, i.e., courts, law enforcement agencies, bar associations, and law schools, together with the judges, prosecutors, police, lawyers, mediators, and legal educators who populate them. The same goes for development assistance intended to improve the performance of these institutions. According to a 2020 US Government Accountability Office report, the vast majority of US rule of law assistance targets justice institutions with training and technical know-how for justice system operators, while just 5% aims to strengthen fairness and access to justice for those who need justice services.[4]

While policy making and development assistance focus on strengthening justice institutions, recent studies of the global justice gap reveal that most people do not turn to these institutions to solve their justice problems. Household surveys conducted by the World Justice Project (WJP) in over 100 countries revealed that roughly half of those surveyed had a legal problem in the preceding two years, yet fewer than one third sought assistance of any kind, and just 17% turned to lawyers, courts, or other institutions for help.[5] The study found that barriers to accessing justice vary, but the most prevalent obstacle is that people do not understand their problems as legal or know that the justice system might provide relief. Less than a third (29%) were able to obtain information, advice, or representation necessary to address their problem.

---

[4] "Rule of Law Assistance: Agency Efforts are Guided by Various Strategies, and Overseas Missions Should Ensure that Programming is Fully Coordinated," GA0-20-393, U.S. Government Accountability Office, June 2020, https://www.gao.gov/products/gao-20-393; *see also* European Commission, Directorate-General for International Partnerships, J. Bossuyt, C. Vaillant, & L. MacKellar, et al., *Evaluation of the European Union Support to Rule of Law and Anticorruption in Partner Countries (2010-2021)* (Publications Office of the European Union, 2022), 12, https://data.europa.eu/doi/10.2841/664918.

[5] "Global Insights on Access to Justice 2019: Findings from the World Justice Project General Population Poll in 101 Countries," The World Justice Project, July 2019, https://worldjusticeproject.org/our-work/research-and-data/global-insights-access-justice-2019.

One in six people reported that it was difficult or nearly impossible to find the money required to solve their legal problem.[6]

These findings underscore that to close the global justice gap, we need to turn justice policy making on its head. Rather than strengthening justice institutions to which people do not turn, we need to focus on understanding people's justice needs and developing policies and services to meet them. Fortunately, this paradigm shift is underway, spurred in no small part by the imperative presented by the SDGs. International organizations, including the United Nations Development Programme, the World Bank, the International Development Law Organization, and the Organization for Economic Cooperation and Development, have embraced people-centered justice.[7] USAID's new Rule of Law Policy, announced during the 2023 Summit for Democracy, "places the individual affected by the law at the core of the policies, institutions, processes, and practices that comprise justice and related systems and services."[8] Meanwhile a growing cohort of governments, international organizations, and civil society organizations have formed the Justice Action Coalition to drive forward a people-centered approach to justice services across the globe.[9]

---

[6] The World Justice Project, "Global Insights on Access to Justice 2019."

[7] Each of these organizations is a member of the Justice Action Coalition, "a multi-stakeholder alliance of countries and organizations that is working to achieve measurable progress on justice for people and communities." See https://www.sdg16.plus/justice-action-coalition/. See also "OECD Framework and Good Practice Principles for People-Centred Justice," GOV/PGC(2021)26 (OECD 2021), https://www.oecd.org/governance/global-roundtables-access-to-justice/good-practice-principles-for-people-centred-justice.pdf; "Diverse Pathways to People-Centred Justice: Report of the Working Group on Customary and Informal Justice and SDG16.3," IDLO, Working Group on Customary and Informal Justice and SDG16+, 2023, https://www.idlo.int/sites/default/files/2023/other/documents/diverse_pathways_to_people-centred_justice_sept_2023.pdf.

[8] "USAID Announced the Rule of Law Policy, the First-Ever U.S. Government Policy Dedicated to Rule of Law Assistance," Press Release, USAID, March 28, 2023, https://www.usaid.gov/news-information/press-releases/mar-28-2023-usaid-announces-rule-law-policy-first-ever-us-government-policy-dedicated-rule-law-assistance.

[9] As of November 2023, the Coalition comprised 20 governments and 17 partner organizations. Justice Action Coalition website, https://www.justice.sdg16.plus/justice-action-coalition.

Data Gaps and the Need for a Strengthened Justice Data Ecosystem

Policy makers seeking to implement a people-centered approach to justice emphasize the importance of data to understand people's justice needs, map their efforts to solve them, identify the barriers to justice they face, and develop and evaluate effective policy responses.[10] Unfortunately, justice systems are notoriously laggard in gathering, analyzing, and using data. Compared to health or education systems, for example, we know relatively little about the quality of justice institutions' services or their impact on their clientele. Moreover, most of the justice data available to policy makers is administrative data generated by justice institutions, and it therefore fails to capture the experience of the vast majority of people who do not turn to institutions with their justice problems.[11] Data that does exist is often siloed in different justice institutions and collected in ways that are not consistent, comparable, or susceptible to disaggregation by key demographic or geographic dimensions. Finally, many justice institutions lack staff with expertise in data collection and analysis to support the kind of evidence-based approach to policy making that a people-centered approach to justice requires. In sum, justice systems globally suffer from an inadequate supply of and demand for justice data.[12]

---

[10] "Rule of Law Policy: A Renewed Commitment to Justice, Rights, and Security for All," 5, USAID, April 2023, https://www.usaid.gov/sites/default/files/2023-04/USAID%20ROL%20Policy%20508%20230406.pdf ("User-friendly and problem-solving justice, rights, and security interventions are driven by data – about users, societies, needs, problems, processes, experiences, and outcomes. In promoting the rule of law, as in other development assistance efforts, lack of data and other forms of evidence invites failure.")

[11] "Grasping the Justice Gap: Opportunities and Challenges for People-Centered Justice Data," 4, The World Justice Project, Pathfinders for Peaceful, Just, and Inclusive Societies, OECD, 2021, https://worldjusticeproject.org/our-work/publications/working-papers/grasping-justice-gap.

[12] "Disparities, Vulnerability, and Harnessing Data for People-centered Justice," 47–9, The World Justice Project, December 2023, https://worldjusticeproject.org/our-work/research-and-data/wjp-justice-data-graphical-report-ii.

Jurisdictions that are serious about pursuing people-centered justice and closing the justice gap will require a significant investment in data and evidence-based policy making. This cannot be left to any one institution. Rather, to build a robust and effective justice data ecosystem will require coordinated action by diverse actors, including courts, ministries of justice, planning and budget agencies, national statistical offices, bar associations, legal aid associations, social services agencies, and civil society organizations. A network of these entities is required to coordinate the consistent collection of justice data across sectors and institutions and to support policy makers in analyzing and using this data to develop, track, and evaluate innovative justice services that meet people's needs.

Required Innovation in Justice Services

Recent research drawing on legal needs surveys makes clear that traditional justice institutions and actors are failing to meet people's justice needs. Moreover, the size and nature of the justice gap are such that it cannot be closed simply by increasing the number of courts, judges, and lawyers or otherwise expanding existing justice services. In a 2016 study, the ABA Commission on the Future of Legal Services concluded that decades of efforts to expand free legal aid and promote pro bono legal services have done little to close the justice gap in the United States.[13] As Professor Rebecca Sandefur has convincingly argued, such efforts to close the justice gap with more legal services are doomed to fall short, because they misconceive the problem as inadequate access to legal services, rather than inadequate access to justice.[14] When we understand the justice gap as the inability of many people to obtain just outcomes, then we can conceive of many potential solutions, only some of which require the involvement of traditional legal services and justice institutions.

---

[13] "A Report on the Future of Legal Services," 5, ABA Commission on the Future of Legal Services (ABA) 2016, https://www.americanbar.org/content/dam/aba/administrative/center-for-innovation/2016-fls-final-report.pdf.

[14] Rebecca Sandefur, "Access to What?" *Daedalus* (Winter 2019): 49–55, https://www.amacad.org/publication/access-what.

Reconceiving the justice gap in these terms underscores the importance of innovation in justice services to achieve access to justice for all. Drawing on design thinking, legal innovators have made important strides in recent years to rethink justice services to better meet people's justice needs.[15] Such innovation can take many forms and involve diverse actors. Some types of justice problems may lend themselves to effective preventive interventions to head off problems before they emerge or become acute. Systemic reforms that clarify rights, create expedited procedures, or shift burdens of proof may help eliminate a whole class of disputes or facilitate their swift resolution.[16] A Washington, DC Access to Justice Commission study of probate law and practice is illustrative of such innovation. The Commission recommended simplifying the process and expanding the use of non-judicial administrative procedures, particularly in small estate cases valued at less than $80,000, the swift and efficient resolution of which can have significant impacts on a family's housing tenure, wealth, and well-being. The vast majority (97%) of small estate cases in Washington, DC, involve self-represented individuals, so a simplified administrative procedure can go a long way toward achieving just outcomes.[17]

In other cases, just outcomes may be reached through alternative dispute resolution, informal justice mechanisms, or paralegal or other non-lawyer assistance. For example, in a 2021 study, the World Justice Project documented the effectiveness of alternative justice centers serving indigenous communities in Hidalgo state in

---

[15] See, e.g., Justice Innovation, Stanford Legal Design Lab, https://justice-innovation.law.stanford.edu.

[16] Rebecca Sandefur, "Access to What?" *Daedalus* (Winter 2019): 53, https:// www.amacad.org/publication/access-what.

[17] "Strengthening Probate Administration in the District of Columbia," District of Columbia Access to Justice Commission, DC Estate Administration Working Group, February 2022, https://dcaccesstojustice.org/wp-content/uploads/2022/02/Strengthening-Probate-Administration-in-DC-Feb-2022.pdf. At the time of the study, the District of Columbia defined small estates as those valued at less than $40,000; the Commission recommended expanding application of expedited administrative procedures to all estates valued at less than $80,000.

Mexico. Indigenous mediators, trained by the state justice institutions and trusted by the local population, were able to facilitate processes by which parties to disputes identify solutions they find acceptable and just. These centers have proven particularly effective in reaching women and girls who struggle to obtain justice through formal justice institutions, and more than 85% of cases were successfully concluded with an agreed resolution between the parties, with high levels of satisfaction reported by participants.[18] Justice service providers in many jurisdictions have innovated effectively by co-locating legal services with other social services, enabling a holistic, problem-solving approach that helps not only resolve the immediate legal problem but also address root causes or negative consequences that relate to it.[19]

Given the significant proportion of those with justice needs who do not understand their problems as legal, information and education about legal rights, responsibilities, and resolution options can be transformative innovations in justice service delivery. Recent years have seen impactful efforts across a wide range of communication channels and initiatives to get critical legal information and advice in the hands of those with justice needs. Among these innovations are the creative use of non-lawyer assistance (e.g., paralegals, allied legal professionals, non-lawyer court navigators, and even generative AI) and unbundled legal services, enabling consumers to engage lawyers for particular aspects of case representation for which they need and can afford assistance.[20] In many

---

[18] "Mediacion indigena," World Justice Project, November 2021, https://worldjusticeproject.mx/wp-content/uploads/2021/11/Reporte-Mediacio%CC%81n-Indi%CC%81gena.pdf.

[19] See infra n. 27 and accompanying text.

[20] Namati's global network of grassroots legal empowerment paralegals is a particularly noteworthy example of this type of innovation. See generally, https://namati.org/; Michael Houlberg & Nathalie Anne Knowlton, *Allied Legal Professionals: A National Framework for Program Growth* (Institute for the Advancement of the American Legal System (IAALS), June 2023), https://iaals.du.edu/sites/default/files/documents/publications/alp_national_framework.pdf; Mary E. McClymont, *Nonlawyer Navigators in State Courts: An Emerging Consensus* (The Justice Lab, Georgetown University, June 2019), https://www.ncsc.org/__data/assets/pdf_file/

jurisdictions, such innovations that involve changing *who* provides legal information and advice require changes to laws and regulations that govern the licensing and oversight of the legal profession, and such regulatory reform has proven contentious where the legal profession guards its prerogatives jealously.[21]

Technology provides a growing array of tools to facilitate all of the foregoing types of innovation. Online tools and apps can help people understand their rights and options, access forms, and generate pleadings. As an example, JustFix.org provides such resources and services to those with housing disputes in New York City, serving over 300,000 users in 2021, according to its annual impact report.[22] Formal justice institutions have also embraced technological innovation. Particularly since the COVID-19 pandemic, court-sanctioned online tools are proliferating, in some cases providing full-fledged online dispute resolution platforms that can guide parties to minor disputes through a complete adjudication process that efficiently generates just outcomes, often without needing a lawyer or formal institutional intervention.[23]

While the justice gap remains vast, recent years have seen a dramatic growth in innovation in the delivery of justice services. With the right enabling environment, including financial resources, regulatory reform, and cross-sectoral collaboration, such innovation holds great promise for making inroads on the justice gap in the coming period.

0024/53691/Justice-Lab-Navigator-Report-6.11.19.pdf; Michael Houlberg & Janet Drobinske, *Unbundled Legal Services in the New Normal* (IAALS, September 2022), https://iaals.du.edu/sites/default/files/documents/publications/unbundled_legal_services_new_normal.pdf; Ashwin Telang "The Promise and Peril of AI Legal Services to Equalize Justice," *JOLT Digest* (March 14, 2023), https://jolt.law.harvard.edu/digest/the-promise-and-peril-of-ai-legal-services-to-equalize-justice.

[21] Matt Reynolds, "When it comes to deregulation of the legal industry, divisions run deep," *The ABA Journal* (November 16, 2023), https://www.abajournal.com/web/article/when-it-comes-to-deregulation-of-the-legal-industry-divisions-run-deep.

[22] See generally, JustFix.org. JustFix, 2021 Annual Report, https://drive.google.com/file/d/1RdT2l8bZpd1xmghceO6k2a0HWywfaqln/view.

[23] See, e.g., The Civil Resolution Tribunal of British Columbia, with official jurisdiction over minor civil disputes. https://civilresolutionbc.ca/.

Essential Cross-Sectoral Collaboration to Meet People's Justice Needs

As the foregoing discussion of data initiatives and innovation illustrates and numerous studies confirm, closing the justice gap cannot be left to justice institutions alone. Collaboration among a wide range of justice sector actors and between them and other governmental and nongovernmental actors is essential to gathering and analyzing the data required to understand people's justice needs as well as to devising and implementing innovative, effective policy responses.

Data from legal needs surveys highlight that people do not experience one-dimensional, single-issue justice problems, and solving them often requires navigating a complex system of laws, regulations, and judicial and administrative institutions as well as addressing extant social conditions contributing to or resulting from people's justice problems. Analyzing data from legal needs surveys in over 100 countries, the WJP found that problems relating to housing, employment, family, money, debt, and public services co-occur frequently, with one problem often triggering another. The study found that those with housing problems are 45% more likely to have money and debt problems and at least 29% more likely to have issues with public services, employment, and family disputes.[24] Analysis of the data points to certain root causes or demographic factors that can contribute to or exacerbate justice problems. For example, women and people living in poverty are more likely to lack proof of legal identity or legal documentation confirming land and housing tenure, which in turn increases their vulnerability to rights violations and other justice problems.[25] Numerous studies of criminal justice cases point to the co-occurrence and cascading effect of both civil and

---

[24] "Dissecting the Justice Gap in 104 Countries: Data Graphical Report I," 8, 17, The World Justice Project, July 2023, https://worldjusticeproject.org/our-work/research-and-data/wjp-justice-data-graphical-report-i.

[25] "Disparities, Vulnerability, and Harnessing Data for People-centered Justice," 5, The World Justice Project, December 2023, https://worldjusticeproject.org/our-work/research-and-data/wjp-justice-data-graphical-report-ii.

criminal justice problems, as well as the frequent relevance of other social and health factors, such as domestic violence and substance abuse.[26]

Growing awareness of the multi-faceted nature of people's justice problems and needs has over the past three decades led to a significant amount of innovative, cross-sectoral collaboration in the delivery of justice services. Models and best practices include family justice centers to deliver comprehensive services to victims of domestic violence under one roof; problem-solving courts and other holistic criminal justice services that integrate relevant civil justice and social services to address root causes as well as collateral consequences of involvement with the criminal justice system; and the "multi-door courthouse" model that incorporates alternative dispute resolution as well as social services in court services.[27]

Building and sustaining such collaboration requires buy-in, coordination, and support from diverse institutions and stakeholders. Drawing from its study of effective justice models across the globe, the Hague Institute for Innovation of Law underscores the importance of leadership and recommends that jurisdictions establish a task force with a mission to drive the type of coordination required

---

[26] See, e.g., Kathryne M. Young and Katie R. Billings, "An Intersectional Examination of U.S. Civil Justice Problems," 2023 ULR 487, 512 (2023) (survey respondents who had been arrested were 2.18 times more likely to experience a problem with debt in the past year; survivors of sexual assault or domestic violence were 1.43 times more likely to have debt problems in the past year), https://doi.org/10.26054/0d-zv1c-rh2z.

[27] See, e.g., *A Roadmap to Problem-Solving Courts* (American Bar Association Coalition for Justice (ABA) 2008); Mariana Hernandez-Crespo Gonstead, "A Dialogue between Professors Frank Sander and Mariana Hernandez, 'Exploring the Evolution of the Multi-Door Courthouse (Part One),'" (2008), https://papers.ssrn.com/sol3/papers.cfm?abstract_id=1265221; Thomas Duncan, Ronald Stewart, Kimberly Joseph, Deborah Kuhls, Tracey Dechert, Sharven Taghavi, Stephanie Bonne and Kuzuhide Matsushima, "American Association for the Surgery of Trauma Prevention Committee Review: Family Justice Centers—A Not-So-Novel, But Unknown Gem," *Trauma Surgery Acute Care Open* 6 no. 1 (June 7, 2021): e000725, https://doi.org/10.1136/tsaco-2021-000725.

to implement a people-centered approach to justice services.[28] In the United States, such coordination has been advanced by state-level Access to Justice Commissions and, at the federal level, by the Legal Aid Interagency Roundtable, which is co-chaired by the Attorney General and the Counsel to the President and integrates the access-to-justice work of 28 federal agencies.[29]

Notwithstanding these exemplary efforts to promote multi-sectoral collaboration, the justice sector remains stubbornly siloed and resistant to the holistic approaches required to meet people's justice needs. Too often, a combination of professional specialization, protectionism in the legal guild, and institutional values, such as judicial and prosecutorial independence and legal finality, keep justice sector actors from working together and with other sectors to take data-driven, evidence-based and innovative, problem-solving approaches to meeting people's justice needs. Promising exceptions are emerging across the globe, but a justice sector paradigm shift will be required to close the justice gap. As elaborated in the following section, institutions of higher education are well-positioned to stimulate and sustain this critical shift.

THE ROLE OF HIGHER EDUCATION

Achieving the SDG's promise of "access to justice for all" remains a distant pipe-dream, with an estimated 5.1 billion with unmet justice needs. Progress has been limited as the COVID-19 pandemic, new armed conflicts, and rising authoritarianism have in many jurisdictions exacerbated justice problems and hobbled institutional

---

[28] "Delivering Justice Rigorously: A Guide to People-Centered Justice Programming," 26–33, HiiL, https://dashboard.hiil.org/publications/trend-report-2021-delivering-justice/#:~:text=HiiL's%20mission%20is%20to%20ensure,particular%20type%20of%20justice%20problem.

[29] See generally, "Access to Justice Commissions," American Bar Association, https://www.americanbar.org/groups/legal_aid_indigent_defense/resource_center_for_access_to_justice/atj-commissions/?login; "Legal Aid Inter-agency Roundtable," Office of Access to Justice, U.S. Department of Justice, https://www.justice.gov/atj/legal-aid-interagency-roundtable.

responses. As explained in the foregoing section, reversing these negative trends requires new ways of conceptualizing and delivering justice services, taking a people-centered, problem-solving approach that draws on data about people's justice needs and marshals diverse expertise and policy tools to solve them. This section describes the important role that colleges and universities can play in seeding and supporting this new way of delivering justice, identifying exemplary efforts, and outlining lessons and recommendations that emerge from those experiences.

University Strengths in Data Science, Innovation, and Multidisciplinary Collaboration

Three key elements of the paradigm shift required in justice services are increased use of data and evidence about people's justice problems and what works to solve them; innovation in the delivery of justice services; and cross-sectoral collaboration in support of these objectives. Each of these elements plays to a particular strength in higher education and points to the leadership role that colleges and universities should be playing in efforts to close the justice gap.

First, with respect to tapping data insights relevant to the justice gap, higher education has unique capabilities. Data science has over the past decade been one of the fastest growing fields of study, and many institutions have invested significantly in statistics and related STEM departments and centers to serve as hubs of this activity on campus, in some cases focusing these efforts specifically on justice issues.[30] Institutions of higher education are well-positioned to mobilize state-of-the art faculty expertise and student researcher human resources to gather and analyze data on justice problems and solutions.

Examples of institutions that have undertaken innovative and impactful justice data initiatives abound and can provide

---

[30] See Clint Raine, "The Rise of Data Science and Data Analytics Programs," *Encoura Blog* (September 12, 2023) (finding 900% growth in data science degrees and certificates awarded between 2012 and 2021), https://encoura.org/the-rise-of-data-science-and-data-analytics-programs/.

inspiration for other education leaders. In some cases, universities have contributed to legal needs surveys, which, as noted, are particularly valuable in taking a people-centered, as opposed to a justice institution-centric, approach to understanding justice problems and identifying solutions. Such surveys are resource-intensive, and leveraging university expertise for survey design and data analysis can help make such data collection possible. The WJP Atlas of Legal Needs Surveys, which maps 236 such studies undertaken globally since 1991, includes at least a dozen in which institutions of higher education played a role, often in collaboration with local legal aid providers or access to justice commissions.[31]

As an alternative or complement to legal needs surveys, institutions of higher education can gather and analyze legal, institutional, or administrative data on access to justice issues and contribute resulting insights to relevant policy-making processes. This can take the form of studies mapping regulatory regimes relevant to access to justice, as has been done by the National Center for Access to Justice affiliated with Fordham Law School. Drawing on pro bono legal research as well as surveys of key justice sector stakeholders, its "Justice Index" evaluates, scores, and ranks each US state on the extent to which it has adopted best practices in the laws and rules that govern four dimensions of access to justice: attorney access, self-help access, language access, and disability access.[32] Mapped against legal needs surveys, such data could helpfully reveal correlations between different access to justice policies and people's justice outcomes to make the case for the most effective interventions.

Other institutions have undertaken analysis of administrative or case data to identify disparities in justice outcomes and to evaluate different policies for enhancing access to justice. An example is the

---

[31] "Atlas of Legal Needs Surveys," World Justice Project, https://worldjusticeproject.org/our-work/research-and-data/atlas-legal-needs-surveys. See, e.g., the legal needs survey carried out by the University of Tennessee School of Social Work under contract with the Tennessee Access to Justice Commission and the Tennessee Alliance for Legal Services, Linda M. Dougherty, "Legal Needs Assessment 2014," https://www.tals.org/sites/tals.org/files/2014%20Legal%20Needs%20Assessment.pdf.

[32] "Justice Index," National Center for Access to Justice, https://ncaj.org/state-rankings/justice-index.

work of the Institute for the Quantitative Study of Inclusion, Diversity, and Equity (QSIDE). Led by Williams College Professor Chad Topaz and drawing on contributions from student fellows and the expertise of academic and civil society partners across the United States, QSIDE has built databases and analyzed sentencing, arraignment, and detention decisions by judicial actors. Their findings highlight disparities in judicial decision-making and make the case for greater justice data transparency and judicial accountability.[33] In a similar vein, scholars at the University of Michigan-affiliated think tank Poverty Solutions have launched the Prosecutor Transparency Project, a collaboration with the local prosecutor's office and the American Civil Liberties Union of Michigan to gather and analyze administrative data for potential racial disparities in prosecutors' charging decisions and to generate a public-facing data dashboard.[34] In another compelling example of the valuable access-to-justice insights that such research can provide, scholars at the University of Pennsylvania analyzed administrative data from over a half-million criminal cases to evaluate the impact of holistic legal services – providing clients with interdisciplinary services, such as a social worker and housing advocate, as well as criminal legal defense. Random case assignment between two legal aid organizations – one providing holistic services, the other traditional legal services – created a natural experiment that enabled the researchers to rigorously measure the impact of the holistic approach, finding that holistic services reduced the likelihood of a prison sentence by

---

[33] See, e.g., Oded Oren, Chad M. Topaz, and Courtney M. Oliva, "Cost of Discretion: Judicial Decision-Making, Pretrial Detention, and Public Safety in New York City," *Scrutinize*, Institute for the Quantitative Study of Inclusion, Diversity, and Equity, Zimroth Center on the Administration of Criminal Law (2023), https://www.pretrial.org/files/assets/cost-of-discretion-report.pdf; Maria-Veronica Ciocanel, Chad M. Topaz, Rebecca Santorella, Shilad Sen, Christian Michael Smith, & Adam Hufstetler, "JUSTFAIR: Judicial System Transparency through Federal Archive Inferred Records" (October 26, 2020), https://journals.plos.org/plosone/article?id=10.1371/journal.pone.0241381.

[34] See "Washtenaw County Prosecutor's Office: Racial Equity Study and Criminal Justice Dashboard," Poverty Solutions, https://poverty.umich.edu/faculty-project/washtenaw-county-prosecutors-office-racial-equity-study-and-criminal-justice-dashboard/.

16% and the length of sentences by 24%.[35] While these examples all draw from studies of criminal justice data, scholars can provide data insights on a wide range of civil justice issues as well. Poverty Solutions-affiliated scholars have, for example, undertaken systematic analysis of eviction case data in Michigan, identifying disparities in eviction rates across the state, correlations with various demographic characteristics, and low rates of legal representation among tenants facing eviction, among issues warranting policy makers' attention.[36]

As data science progresses to encompass cutting-edge tools, including the use of artificial intelligence, big data, and web-scraping approaches, the expertise and insights of scholars will be all the more valuable to policy makers grappling with the justice gap. Moreover, colleges and universities, as institutions that are distinct from government and enjoy relative independence from shifting political and policy priorities, can play a critical role in breaking down policy siloes, promoting collaborations, and building and sustaining the inter-institutional data ecosystem required to address the justice gap. They can convene and coordinate relevant stakeholders to gather data in consistent and comparable ways. They can provide critical technical expertise and capacity building to analyze and use justice data where this is lacking among justice sector institutions. Finally, they can also sustain these efforts over time, to generate critical longitudinal findings that can help identify what works in addressing people's justice needs.

As suggested by the foregoing discussion of higher education's role in harnessing data to increase access to justice, academic institutions are also uniquely well-positioned to contribute the multidisciplinary collaboration and innovation that closing the justice

---

[35] James M. Anderson, Maya Buenaventura and Paul Heaton, "The Effects of Holistic Defense on Criminal Justice Outcomes," *Harvard Law Review* 819 (2019), https://harvardlawreview.org/wp-content/uploads/2019/01/819-893_Online.pdf.

[36] See Robert Goodspeed, Kyle Slugg, Margaret Dewar and Elizabeth Benton, "Michigan Evictions: Trends, Data Sources, and Neighborhood Determinants" (May 2020), https://sites.fordschool.umich.edu/poverty2021/files/2021/03/Michigan-Eviction-Project-working-paper-1.pdf.

gap requires. Many of the examples of university data collection and analysis initiatives described here draw on diverse collaborations across research institutions and with government and civil society justice actors, and they are generating and validating new, outside-the-box approaches to delivering justice. Paul Heaton, Academic Director of the Quattrone Center for the Fair Administration of Justice at the University of Pennsylvania Law School, has cited his institution's "low barriers to interdisciplinary cooperation" as critical to his center's impact on justice issues. "For this sort of research to have maximum impact, you need to get a few things right," he explains,

> [y]ou need to marry the technical skill with the institutional knowledge and also need the ability to build partnerships and have access to practitioners, so when you generate new findings, you can take them out and use them to actually make people's lives better.[37]

Universities are research communities rich in diverse expertise to bring to bear on solving the complex systemic problems at the heart of the justice gap. As noted, they have invaluable data science capabilities for collecting, analyzing, and using data to identify justice needs and devise and evaluate effective solutions. Multidisciplinary initiatives can also expose justice policy makers to relevant learning about systemic change in other fields. Professor Heaton argues, for example, that the justice sector can learn from the transportation industry, bringing to the study of miscarriages of justice the same rigor and forward-looking problem solving that transportation safety professionals apply to airline and rail accidents.[38] Others have highlighted the learning that the justice sector could gain from the public health field, particularly in

---

[37] Gyneth K. Shaw, "Game-changing Approach to a Better U.S. Criminal Justice System," *PennToday* (August 19, 2019), https://penntoday.upenn.edu/news/quattrone-center-better-us-criminal-justice-system.

[38] Paul Heaton, "How Transportation Safety Review Can Play a Role In Regulating Law Enforcement," *The Regulatory Review* (February 16, 2017), https://www.theregreview.org/2017/02/16/heaton-transportation-safety-regulating-law-enforcement/.

the use of data and technology and the provision of legal information and non-lawyer services.[39]

Cross-sectoral collaboration in the academy can give rise to new tools, approaches, and partnerships for delivering justice, such as technological innovation, effective communications strategies, or collaboration with cultural, social, education, or health institutions that can help bring justice services to the people who need them. The Stanford Legal Design Lab – a collaboration of Stanford Law School and its "d.school" – is an illustrative example of the creative justice sector problem-solving and systems change that can come from tapping university expertise in law, social science, and technology. Characterized as "an R&D Lab for a better people-centered justice system," the lab has over the past ten years generated dozens of resources and tools for policy makers, court administrators, and other justice sector actors to help close the justice gap.[40] The Center of Law and Technology at Duke University Law School similarly harnesses interdisciplinary applied research to improve justice services, including through courses in design thinking, a "Law Tech Lab," and "Legal Design Derby" competition.[41] Another inspiring example comes from Georgetown University Law Center's Institute for Technology Law and Policy, which has recently launched an ambitious new Judicial Innovation Fellowship for technology industry fellows to work with partner courts to leverage technology, improve justice services, and generate replicable models for use in other jurisdictions.[42] Technology is not the only source of innovation, as demonstrated by a project of Northeastern Law School's East Boston Spatial Justice Lab. Funded by the National Endowment for the Arts, it draws on expertise

---

[39] See "Interview with Sam Muller, Founder and CEO of HiiL," *Josef*, September 16, 2020, https://joseflegal.com/blog/interview-with-dr-sam-muller/.
[40] See generally, https://www.legaltechdesign.com/, Stanford Legal Design Lab.
[41] See generally, Duke Law School, Center on Law and Technology, https://law.duke.edu/dclt/initiatives.
[42] Jason Tashea, "The Judicial Innovation Fellowship: A Roadmap to Strengthen State, Local, Territorial, and Tribal Courts" (February 2023), https://www.law.georgetown.edu/tech-institute/wp-content/uploads/sites/42/2023/02/Judicial-Innovation-Fellowship-Roadmap-1.pdf.

in art, design, law, community organizing, and program evaluation to explore how arts events can build social cohesion and promote more just outcomes.[43] Such initiatives demonstrate the exciting opportunities for change-making innovation through university-led interdisciplinary initiatives to address the justice gap.

Lessons Learned and Recommendations for Higher Education Initiatives to Close the Justice Gap

As highlighted in the foregoing discussion, there is a great need for a transformation of justice services, bringing new data-driven, evidence-based, innovative, and cross-sectoral approaches to meeting people's justice needs. Institutions of higher education are well-equipped to lead this change, and many are already doing so. Review of these existing efforts to increase access to justice yields several lessons learned and recommendations for colleges and universities to consider as they develop initiatives in this area.

Incorporate Collaboration with Affected Communities and Policymakers from the Start. To maximize the policy relevance and eventual uptake of research findings by policymakers, it is important to engage with key policy actors from the design phase of university research initiatives. This ensures that research takes advantage of existing data, addresses real-world policy challenges, and has buy-in from the actors whom the research aims to influence.[44] The most effective university initiatives cited in this chapter involved close consultation between university researchers, affected communities, and policymakers to co-create research and develop and implement collaborative solutions.

Intentionally Build in Learning Opportunities for Students. The transformation of justice systems will require not just research insights from established scholars but also the development of a new generation of justice system actors and policy makers trained

---

[43] See, "National Endowment for the Arts Awards $150,000 grant to Northeastern Law's NuLawLab," https://law.northeastern.edu/nulawlab-awarded-nea-grant/.

[44] Author Interview with Chad Topaz, Co-founder, QSIDE Institute, April 13, 2023.

to bring multi-disciplinary and innovative approaches to justice system strengthening. Building this cohort is an important contribution that higher education can make to closing the justice gap. University initiatives to address justice gap issues should incorporate educational opportunities for students and young scholars. Models abound among the initiatives profiled in this chapter. They include curricular innovations, such as the justice design labs at Stanford and Duke, or the Big Data for Justice Summer Institute at UCLA[45]; student fellowships and research opportunities, such as are enjoyed by the QSIDE Institute fellows[46]; and research conferences and competitions to which students can contribute, such as the Duke Legal Design Derby and the QSIDE Institute's annual Data for Justice conference.

Build Interdisciplinary and Quantitative Skills Among Law Students. A particular focus for educational innovation should be the development of social science skills, including the capacity for quantitative analysis, among law students, many of whom will eventually assume leadership roles in justice institutions. While some schools are incorporating such learning opportunities in law school curricula, much more can be done to keep pace with the rapidly developing data science field. A recent literature review on data science education mapped significant scholarship about innovation in teaching data science to diverse professionals, including in the fields of health, education, business, and environmental science.[47] Notably missing were studies of innovation in teaching data science to legal professionals. This is a gap in legal education that urgently needs to be filled. Promising models include opportunities for joint degrees, certificate programs, or coursework in complementary disciplines for law students, as well as specialized interdisciplinary centers within law schools, such as the Center for Law

---

[45] Big Data for Justice Summer Institute, UCLA, https://bunchecenter.ucla.edu/programs-events/thurgood-marshall-lecture-2/.

[46] QSIDE Institute, Fellowship Program, https://qsideinstitute.org/get-involved/fellowship-program/.

[47] K. Mike, B. Kimelfeld, and O. Hazzan, "The Birth of a New Discipline: Data Science Education," *Harvard Data Science Review* 5, no. 4 (2023). https://doi.org/10.1162/99608f92.280afe66.

and Technology at Duke Law School, or the Quattrone Center for the Fair Administration of Justice at the University of Pennsylvania Law School. Such approaches are essential to equipping law students to be the future transformational leaders of justice systems we need to close the justice gap.

Connect University Justice Initiatives to Global Agendas, including the International Human Rights Movement and the SDG Process. While a number of university initiatives such as those profiled in this chapter are bringing higher education resources to bear on the justice gap challenge, few of these programs are explicitly framed in terms of or connected to relevant global policy agendas, such as the international human rights movement or the SDG process.[48] This is a missed opportunity to strengthen the research and educational experience by bringing to bear comparative approaches and best practices, global datasets, and international standards. Connecting individual institutional efforts to global processes such as the SDGs creates opportunities to pool research capacity and build a shared research agenda across institutions and jurisdictions to reach common goals. The American Bar Foundation's Justice Data Observatory initiative is an illustrative example of the benefits of such an approach, knitting together diverse partners across institutions to develop a shared research agenda with specific reference to implications for the SDG effort.[49] Framing university access to justice initiatives in terms of global policy agendas also provides

---

[48] A notable exception is the work under way at Carnegie Mellon University, the first and now one of a number of institutions of higher education that has undertaken a "Voluntary University Review" of its contributions to the SDGs and specifically framed courses on justice issues in SDG terms. See Carnegie Mellon University, Sustainability Initiative, "2022 Voluntary University Review of the Sustainable Development Goals," https://www.cmu.edu/leadership/the-provost/provost-priorities/sustainability-initiative/cmu-vur-2022.pdf. Some of the legal design work also incorporates human rights reference-points, but these approaches are not mainstreamed in the human rights movement nor are human rights norms central to legal design thinking.

[49] See generally, American Bar Foundation Justice Data Observatory, "People-centered Access to Justice Research: A Global Perspective," 15, https://www.americanbarfoundation.org/wp-content/uploads/2023/11/People-Centered-Access-to-Justice-Research-A-Global-Perspective.pdf.

students with valuable exposure to transnational policy processes and can help prepare them to be effective global citizens. Finally, connecting to global policy processes promises a broader impact of university research, which can reverberate beyond the immediate local policy context and become a global reference point for insights and best practices on closing the justice gap.

CONCLUSION: THE OPPORTUNITY FOR THE HUMAN RIGHTS MOVEMENT

As detailed in this chapter, there is an enormous need for new approaches to solving people's justice problems. Mobilizing institutions of higher education is a key strategy for meeting this need, bringing to bear their multidisciplinary expertise, particularly with respect to data science, as well as their capacity to foster innovation and build multi-sectoral collaboration to transform the delivery of justice services. While tapping universities for this cause promises major dividends for efforts to close the justice gap and achieve SDG16's objective of "access to justice for all," it can also help provide the international human rights movement with new tools, strategies, champions, and constituencies.

As described elsewhere in this volume, recent years have seen a backlash against the mainstream international human rights movement, in particular its focus on civil and political rights and its preoccupation with legal tools and strategies perceived to advance specialized minority interests while neglecting economic rights and interests resonant with broader publics. Both the Universal Declaration of Human Rights and the International Covenant on Civil and Political Rights enshrine the right to an effective remedy for violations of human rights. In modern human rights practice, this right has most often been conceptualized and advanced as a remedy for a particular individualized violation of civil and political rights, delivered through an adjudicated legal process, often before a national or international court. Such legal processes typically focus narrowly on obtaining justice for the particular litigants to the case. Sometimes this litigation can generate systemic change to address the injustices of which the particular case is illustrative.

But rarely can it provide a solution to the broad social and economic issues that frequently contribute to or result from injustices.

Reconceived as a societal commitment to close the justice gap, however, the right to a remedy takes on a different cast and is susceptible to a broader set of strategies for its vindication. Abandoning a narrow, legalistic framework for the right to a remedy and bringing the problem-solving tools of social science, data science, and systemic policymaking to bear could be transformative for the human rights movement. Data analysis of the injustices people confront can highlight different dimensions of their problems and the barriers to solving them they face. Multi-sectoral collaboration and problem-solving that harnesses technology and other innovative tools can generate remedies for thousands – even millions – of such problems, often without setting foot in a courtroom.

The SDGs – with their broad agenda, encompassing economic and social rights, and emphasizing data-driven approaches and cross-sectoral collaboration – provide a particularly valuable framework for developing such a new approach to human rights. Doing so promises to bring experts from diverse academic and professional disciplines to join ranks with the lawyers who have dominated the human rights movement in recent decades. Claiming credit for closing even a fraction of the global justice gap affecting 5.1 billion people would go a long way to building much-needed popular support for the embattled human rights movement.

3

JUDICIAL INSTITUTIONS, SDGs, AND THE 2030 AGENDA ACROSS LATIN AMERICA AND THE CARIBBEAN

Alvaro Herrero

International Open Justice Network, Argentina

ABSTRACT

This chapter analyzes the state of localization of the Sustainable Development Goals (SDGs) by the judiciary in Latin America and the Caribbean, arguing that while important and promising progress has been made in the region, there are still numerous barriers that limit the progress of the 2030 Agenda in the justice sector. It argues that while SDG 16 was the entry point for this agenda, justice systems are gradually broadening their focus and addressing other SDGs. It also highlights the importance of higher education institutions, such as law, public policy and social science schools, in driving a cultural shift within justice sector institutions toward strengthening both knowledge and implementation of the SDGs. The chapter also provides numerous examples of experiences with the implementation of the SDGs by judiciaries and supranational institutions related to the justice sector, showcasing the expansion of this agenda in the sector beyond traditional institutions. Some of the barriers to greater progress in the 2030 Agenda in the justice sector are a product of the culture of judicial institutions, their lack of public management capacity, the absence of monitoring and evaluation, and the limited application of digital tools that allow one to take advantage of the value of data and new technologies. Finally, the chapter notes that the recent advancement of the open justice paradigm and the transformation of the curricula of higher education institutions are two clear opportunities in the medium term to increase the involvement of the judiciary in the SDGs.

Keywords: 2030 Agenda; judiciary; justice; SDG 16; law schools; open justice

INTRODUCTION

The main objective of this chapter is to evaluate the different possibilities for the judiciary to address the Sustainable Development Goals (SDGs). The SDGs were originally conceived as an agenda with targets and indicators to guide, orient, and coordinate the efforts of countries to achieve sustainable development. In any given country, this generally falls to the executive branch, which designs policies, allocates resources, implements projects and evaluates results. However, the range of actors involved in the implementation of the SDGs has rapidly expanded. Local governments, such as cities, provinces and subnational governments in general, joined the 2030 Agenda endeavor, articulating efforts to localize the SDGs and align their government plans with the goals and indicators designed by the United Nations. This gradually included other state actors that began to think about how to contribute to the achievement of the SDGs, such as Supreme Audit Institutions and ombudsmen, among others. Institutions of higher education, as well as the private sector, have also played roles in advancing the SDGs.

The SDGs have, in fact, gradually become the common language that brings together all international and regional spheres of debate and policy advocacy associated with sustainable development.

Thus, conferences related to issues such as education, environment, health, urban development, gender, and poverty, among others, have begun to be framed and organized within the conceptual framework of the SDGs, their targets, and indicators. The language of the SDGs thus has become a common tool in the field of sustainable development, with high levels of impact and effectiveness.

In this context, the two factors mentioned above, the broadening of actors and the universalization of the SDGs as a common language in the world of sustainable development, influenced the judiciaries and justice sector institutions to begin to feel challenged and attracted by this agenda, characterized for the most part by language, tools, and methods foreign to the daily practice of judicial institutions. Despite their lack of familiarity with the global agenda of sustainable development, justice sector leaders were attracted to this new global project to promote inclusive, sustainable and leave-no-one-behind development.

The following sections analyze the process by which the judiciaries became involved with the SDGs and the 2030 Agenda, what were the most common lines of work, and what are the gaps and opportunities to deepen the work of justice sector institutions in this field. They also explore the potential role of higher education institutions, such as law and social science schools, in raising the awareness and knowledge of both the judiciary and today's law students, who are the future members of the judiciary, on development and human rights issues, thereby engaging them in a rights-based and/or public administration approach to the SDGs.

JUDICIARIES AND THE SDGs

Justice sector institutions encompass a broad range of entities including courts, law enforcement agencies, prosecutors, public defenders, prisons and correctional facilities, legal aid organizations, anti-corruption agencies, and oversight bodies. Their entry point into the 2030 Agenda has usually been SDG 16. Goal 16 is about promoting peaceful and inclusive societies, providing access to justice for all and building effective, accountable, and inclusive institutions at all levels.[1] It is based on the premise that people everywhere should be free from fear of all forms of violence and feel safe in their lives, regardless of their ethnicity, faith or sexual orientation, and should live in peaceful societies and enjoy equal access to justice, ensuring that vulnerable populations are not marginalized or abused. In addition, Goal 16 aligns with the broader human rights framework by promoting societies that respect and uphold individual rights, as well as the right to privacy, freedom of expression, and access to information. In short, this goal is closely intertwined with the functioning of justice sector institutions, as they play a pivotal role in upholding the rule of law, ensuring access to justice, and combating various forms of injustice, including corruption and human rights abuses. Given its focus on strengthening institutions, SDG16 is considered to have a facilitating or enabling role in the implementation of all the SDGs.

Below are the SDG 16 targets:

- 16.1 Significantly reduce all forms of violence and related death rates everywhere;

- 16.2 End abuse, exploitation, trafficking, and all forms of violence against and torture of children;

- 16.3 Promote the rule of law at the national and international levels, and ensure equal access to justice for all;

- 16.4 By 2030, significantly reduce illicit financial and arms flows, strengthen the recovery and return of stolen assets and combat all forms of organized crime;

- 16.5 Substantially reduce corruption and bribery in all their forms;

- 16.6 Develop effective, accountable, and transparent institutions at all levels;

- 16.7 Ensure responsive, inclusive, participatory, and representative decision-making at all levels;

---

[1] See "Global progress report on Sustainable Development Goal 16 indicators: A wake-up call for action on peace, justice and inclusion," UNODOC, UNOHCHR, UNDP, September 21, 2023, https://www.undp.org/publications/global-progress-report-sustainable-development-goal-16-indicators-wake-call-action-peace-justice-and-inclusion.

- 16.8 Broaden and strengthen the participation of developing countries in the institutions of global governance;

- 16.9 By 2030, provide legal identity for all, including birth registration;

- 16.10 Ensure public access to information and protect fundamental freedoms, in accordance with national legislation and international agreements;

- 16.A Strengthen relevant national institutions, including through international cooperation, for building capacity at all levels, in particular in developing countries, to prevent violence and combat terrorism and crime;

- 16.B Promote and enforce non-discriminatory laws and policies for sustainable development.[2]

Justice sector institutions are instrumental in achieving the SDG 16 targets, as they are responsible for enforcing laws, protecting human rights, promoting transparency, and fostering citizen participation in decision-making processes. However, for the actions of justice sector institutions to be effective and contribute to the achievement of these targets, they must act in a coordinated manner and with a strategy that encompasses them, as the underlying problems are complex, in many cases multi-causal, and difficult to solve. For this reason, in practice, in Latin America and the Caribbean, most of the policies designed to address the challenging issues contained in SDG 16 are often led by the executive branch. The majority of initiatives come from Executive Branch agencies, such as ministries of justice, ministries of public security, access to justice programs, transparency and/or anti-corruption offices, among others.[3] Moreover, given its focus on promoting effective, inclusive institutions at all levels, SDG 16 is seen as playing an

---

[2] See https://www.globalgoals.org/goals/16-peace-justice-and-strong-institutions/.

[3] See for example the experience of Buenos Aires city in localizing SDG 16. https://www.undp.org/es/argentina/publicaciones/hacia-un-gobierno-abierto-el-proceso-de-adaptacion-del-ods-16-en-la-ciudad-autonoma-de-buenos-aires.

instrumental role as an accelerator of the overall SDG framework, and thus its rule of law and rights-oriented side tends to be overshadowed by its non-judicial, institution-oriented dimension.

In Latin America, the most outstanding SDG 16 reforms, monitoring initiatives, and projects have not been led by the judiciary but by the executive branch, both at the national and subnational levels (i.e., governors and mayors). In turn, many of them relied on the participation and active support of the United Nations Development Program (UNDP), which became the driving force in the design of innovative projects for the localization and monitoring of SDG 16 through research and pilot initiatives.[4] Some of those pilot programs, which included initiatives in Tunisia, Senegal, El Salvador, Uruguay, Indonesia, and Mexico, among others, usually comprised of objectives such as developing and implementing inclusive monitoring methodologies that engage both government and civil society; making the monitoring process open and transparent and ensuring that data was publicly accessible; and using an inclusive approach to SDG16 monitoring to propel implementation, by engaging stakeholders not only in monitoring but also in identifying solutions to the challenges revealed in the reporting. UNDP also supported localization initiatives. For example, in 2018, the UNDP office in Argentina and the government of the city of Buenos Aires implemented an innovative project aimed at measuring SDG 16, particularly the dimensions related to open government, one of the strategic axes of the government's strategic priorities (targets 16.5, 16.6, 16.7 and 16.10).[5] These initiatives, while focused on SDG 16,

---

[4] See for example "the SDG 16 National Monitoring Initiative," an initiative implemented between 2017 and 2021 aimed at supporting more than 10 countries in monitoring SDG 16 using a three-step methodology. Initiated by UNDP, the pilot initiative later became part of the Global Alliance for Reporting Progress on Peaceful, Just and Inclusive Societies and was taken forward in partnership with UNOHCHR, UNESCO, UNHCR, UNODC, UN Women, the UN Global Compact, the TAP Network, and the law firm of White & Case.

[5] More information is available at https://www.undp.org/es/argentina/publications/hacia-un-gobierno-abierto-el-proceso-de-adaptaci%C3%B3n-del-ods-16-en-la-ciudad-aut%C3%B3noma-de-buenos-aires.

were neither led by justice sector institutions nor focused primarily on justice-related issues.

STATE OF THE ART

Nevertheless, the judiciary has gradually begun to explore the range of possibilities offered by SDG 16. On the one hand, the familiarity of judicial institutions with the 2030 Agenda, including the SDGs, their discourse, and SDG methodology, has increased. This is evident when reviewing the judiciaries' communication strategies, as well as its institutional documents and strategic plans, where a greater presence of content or references related to the SDGs can be found.[6] On the other hand, some judiciaries have already incorporated specific programs on the SDGs or are participating along with other branches of government, in efforts to localize and monitor the 2030 Agenda.[7] Some examples from the Latin America and Caribbean region are discussed here.

In **Costa Rica,** in 2016, the judiciary, together with the highest authorities of the executive and legislative branches, signed the National Pact for the Advancement of the SDGs within the framework of the 2030 Agenda for Sustainable Development. In doing so, it committed to (i) incorporate the SDGs and targets that the country has committed to in the 2030 Agenda into the planning and budgeting instruments of the judiciary; (ii) strengthen institutional capacities for the development of policies, plans, programs and projects for the implementation and monitoring of the SDG targets; and (iii) be accountable to the public on the progress and gaps in the implementation of the targets related to the SDGs.[8]

---

[6] See for example the strategic plans of Costa Rica's Supreme Court of Justice, accessed May 15, 2024, https://planificacion.poder-judicial.go.cr/index.php/estrategia/plan-estrategico-institucional, and Dominican Republic, https://transparencia.poderjudicial.gob.do/transparencia/info?IdContenido=1210.

[7] See for example the case of Costa Rica, https://www.mideplan.go.cr/poder-judicial-alineado-con-los-ods.

[8] More information available at https://ods.cr/es/recursos/noticias/poder-judicial-alineado-con-los-ods.

Interestingly, the Supreme Court made a link between the goals defined by the State of Costa Rica and the guidelines and objectives of the Judiciary's Strategic Institutional Plan.[9] In this way, it adopted a comprehensive approach to the SDGs, articulating its strategic plan with the broad scope of the SDGs as a whole, going beyond the classic approach of many judiciaries, which tend to focus exclusively on SDG 16.

The **Brazilian** judiciary has also been working intensively on the 2030 Agenda and the SDGs. It has been a pioneer in the region in the institutionalization of the 2030 Agenda in its strategic planning. In 2019, the Inter-Ministerial Committee for the 2030 Agenda in the Judiciary was created. In addition, a set of 12 *national* strategic goals for the federal judiciary was approved, including Goal 9 that focused on integrating the 2030 Agenda in the judiciary at all levels of the justice system. Specifically, this Brazilian Goal 9 proposed actions to prevent excessive judicialization of conflicts and to reduce litigation, which resulted in the indexing of a database of 80 million judicial processes for each of the 17 SDGs. Moreover, the Supreme Court established programs aimed at reducing gender inequalities (SDG 5) by balancing opportunities for men and women in the judiciary at all levels, and at promoting the more sustainable use of transportation and more efficient energy consumption (SDG 12) through the implementation of a solar plant for electricity generation to provide for clean and affordable energy solutions.[10]

In **Mexico,** the Electoral Tribunal of the Federal Judiciary maintains a permanent mechanism with the United Nations through various offices and programs, in accordance with the SDGs.[11] Since 2016, it has collaborated with the UNDP in the study, design, implementation, and monitoring of a series of initiatives and

---

[9] See "Institutional Strategic Plan of the Judicial Branch of Costa Rica 2019-2024" (in Spanish), https://pei.poder-judicial.go.cr/index.php/planes?download=9:plan-estrategico-2019-2024-pdf.

[10] More information available at https://www.cnj.jus.br/programas-e-acoes/agenda-2030/como-se-deu-o-historico-de-institucionalizacao-da-agenda-2030-no-poder-judiciario/.

[11] More information available at https://www.te.gob.mx/vinculacion_estrategica/front/coi/gubernamentales/6.

institutional projects that contribute, in particular, to the achievement of SDG 10, on the reduction of inequalities, and SDG 16, on peace, justice and strong institutions.

The Supreme Court of the **Dominican Republic** has incorporated the language of the SDGs and references to the development strategy of the 2030 Agenda. For example, its Strategic Plan 2020–2024 includes references to Target 1.4 of SDG 1, which states that it must "ensure that all men and women, especially the poor and vulnerable, have equal rights to economic resources and access to basic services." It also makes several references to the importance of the SDGs in a global context, particularly SDG 16 for justice sector institutions. However, it does not have an integrated program in relation to the 2030 Agenda and the SDGs.[12]

In the province of Chaco, **Argentina,** the State Supreme Court, together with the executive and legislative branches, implemented a joint strategy to advance the 2030 Agenda. In this context, the head of the judiciary undertook a training and sensitization plan on the nature and implications of the SDGs and later identified a set of specific goals and targets to be prioritized in the judiciary's efforts to implement the 2030 Agenda, including SDGs 1, 3, 4, 5, 10, 11, and 16.[13]

In addition, some institutions related to the justice sector have highlighted the importance of the involvement of judiciaries in the 2030 Agenda. For example, the Ibero-American Commission of Judicial Ethics has advocated for a strong involvement of the judiciary in the implementation of the SDGs. It is considered that justice systems are essential parts of the state and the most obvious recipients of Goal 16 and its targets. Therefore, it is incumbent upon justice systems to align their resources and development plans with the goals of the 2030 Agenda.[14]

---

[12] https://transparencia.poderjudicial.gob.do/transparencia/info?IdContenido=1210

[13] See "Voluntary Local Report 2021," https://sdgs.un.org/sites/default/files/vlrs/2022-12/chaco.pdf.

[14] "The Judiciary and Judges in the face of the 2030 Sustainable Development Goals," Resolution adopted by the Ibero-American Commission on Judicial Ethics in Santo Domingo, Dominican Republic, March 2018, https://www.poderjudicial.es.

In 2018, the Ibero-American Judicial Summit of Supreme Courts issued a declaration to promote the SDGs within the judiciary.[15] Its main recommendations were:

(i) Urge Ibero-American judicial systems to consider and incorporate the objectives of Goal 16 in the development of public policies;
(ii) Promote the incorporation of the SDGs in planning and programming instruments aimed at improving access to justice for all; and
(iii) Promote the dissemination of the Goal 16 targets and their ownership by society.

For its part, the **Judicial Council of Central America and the Caribbean** has created the Specialized Working Group on the SDGs. Its main objective is to promote the implementation of the SDGs in the judiciary.[16] The Council has issued several statements and reports to promote international cooperation and the formation of partnerships between international organizations and justice sector institutions to advance the 2030 Agenda, and to disseminate the SDGs in the judiciary and the Supreme Court.[17]

Other UN agencies have also deployed efforts to increase the engagement of judiciaries in the implementation of SDGs. For example, UNESCO published a guide for judicial operators aimed at advancing the involvement of judicial leadership in the implementation of the 2030 Agenda.[18] Drawing on testimonies from the Supreme Court justices and rule of law experts, the guide includes practical recommendations for the localization of SDG16, with a strong focus on transparency and access to public information.

---

[15] https://www.poderjudicial.gob.ni/genero/pdf/doc_rel_discursos_cumbre/2016_2018_declaraciones/5e_Anexo_5_Declaracion_Objetivos.pdf
[16] https://consejojudicialcc.org/grupos-especializados-de-trabajo/objetivos-de-desarrollo-sostenible/
[17] See https://consejojudicialcc.org/wp-content/uploads/2023/10/Declaracion-sobre-los-Objetivos-de-Desarrollo-Sostenible-en-el-CJCC.pdf.
[18] Javier Benech, "Guía para operadores judiciales sobre la Agenda 2030 para el Desarrollo Sostenible con énfasis en el ODS 16," UNESCO Office Montevideo and Regional Bureau for Science in Latin America and the Caribbean, Uruguay, 2017.

The experiences outlined here show that actual progress in the implementation of the 2030 Agenda in the justice sector is still uneven. Although there are several noteworthy initiatives, there remains a gap in both quantitative and qualitative terms. The number of judiciaries that are deeply engaged in the implementation of the SDGs is still low. Very few Supreme Courts have specific programs to advance the 2030 Agenda. In most cases, judicial institutions are sympathetic to this agenda but do not make systematic efforts or allocate budgetary or human resources. On a positive note, it is worth noting that in Latin America, supranational judicial institutions such as the Ibero-American Judicial Summit and the Central American and Caribbean Judicial Council are increasingly engaged in promoting and disseminating the SDGs, which is a promising sign of interest and potential commitment to this agenda.

The models used so far by the judiciary to promote the SDGs fall into two categories. The first is to use SDG 16 as the backbone of the link between justice sector institutions and the 2030 Agenda. Thus, SDG 16 is the sole focus of the targets, linking justice initiatives primarily to issues such as access to justice, reducing violence, homicides, victims of trafficking, preventing the exploitation of children, and reducing bribery, corruption, and persons deprived of their liberty without a conviction. This approach indicates a bias toward the 2030 Agenda, considering it as a sustainable development agenda that is alien to the judiciary, with the exception of SDG 16. In other words, this vision suggests that only the issues articulated around SDG 16 would be subject to the intervention or responsibility of judicial institutions. Moreover, it could be argued that this vision implies a limited self-perception of the judiciary in the functioning of the state, limiting its role or intervention to handling conflicts, legal matters or jurisdictional issues.

The second model consists of a broader engagement of the judiciary with the development agenda, which is reflected in localization initiatives with a wide range of goals linked to a broader set of SDGs. There is no longer an exclusive focus on SDG 16, but rather the 2030 Agenda is approached as a comprehensive roadmap for development in which judicial institutions have a responsibility.

The underlying premise is an understanding of the judiciary as a branch of government, with broad responsibilities shared with the other branches, and a vision of judicial institutions that goes beyond conflict resolution.

OVERCOMING DIFFICULTIES AND CHALLENGES

A number of factors can be identified that work against deep, sustained, and comprehensive engagement of the justice sector with the SDGs. Most of them are related to aspects of institutional values, institutional capacity, and management models of justice sector institutions. Here, I offer an analysis of the main obstacles that delay or prevent the judiciary from making greater progress on the 2030 Agenda as well as suggestions for shifting cultures. To that end, there is a specific role that higher education institutions can play.

The perceptions of judicial authorities limiting their role in development issues

Within judicial institutions, there tends to be a very limited conception of their institutional and political roles. This implies limited activity in everything that is not strictly related to the administration of justice, i.e., the functioning of the courts and the resolution of conflicts. As a result, leadership of the justice sector is self-limiting or limited in its involvement to issues that affect society or require the participation of all branches of government. In this regard, the 2030 Agenda and the SDGs are clear examples of issues that can be the subject of attention and work by the justice sector, as long as the judicial authorities have a broad and proactive vision of the role of the judiciary in the political system. To change this perception, will likely take a broadening of education on the SDGs in feeder schools to the judiciaries.

A reluctance to engage in projects with the Executive Branch

One of the institutional responses to attempts to concentrate power or the abuse of constitutional powers is the ability of the courts to monitor the other branches' compliance with the constitution, i.e., judicial review. Supreme Courts and Constitutional Courts have the prerogative to control whether the acts, decrees and laws of the legislative and executive branches follow the rules of the game established by the relevant Constitution.

To perform this role with legitimacy and credibility, the judiciary must act impartially and independently. Therefore, members of the Supreme Court and other high courts shall avoid being in situations that could raise doubts about their independence and impartiality or be interpreted as improper approaches to the other branches of government. For this reason, judges tend to remain aloof from political power and avoid frequent contact with government officials, legislators, or representatives of political parties. Thus, over time, this concern for preserving the independence of judicial institutions has created a culture in which the judiciary tends to minimize its interaction with the other branches of government and, with few exceptions, avoids involvement in joint or cooperative projects. As a result, the judiciary often undertakes autonomous projects and operates in isolation from the rest of state institutions.

This institutional reluctance to work or interact with the Executive Branch may partially explain the low-level engagement by judiciaries in advancing the 2030 Agenda beyond rhetoric. Focal points for the implementation and monitoring of this agenda are usually located in the Executive Branch. They are also usually responsible for preparing and coordinating the Voluntary National Reviews (VNRs).[19] This is also the case for Voluntary Local Reviews (VLRs) that are typically prepared and/or coordinated by the Executive Branches of local or subnational governments, such as the mayor's office.[20] Therefore, the prominence of the central sectors of government in promoting, coordinating, and monitoring the commitments made under the 2030 Agenda is undoubtedly a factor that

---

[19] The VNR is a process and product in which countries take stock and assess progress and challenges in the implementation of the Sustainable Development Goals (SDGs) of the 2030 Agenda at the national level.

[20] The VLR is a process and product in which local and regional governments (LRGs) assess their progress towards implementing the 2030 Agenda and the SDGs.

discourages judicial institutions from becoming more involved. Instead of seeking common work-paces, opportunities for coordination and interaction, and platforms to strengthen joint efforts, judicial institutions tend to design their own roadmaps and pathways for their strategies to promote the SDGs. Again, there could be useful ways in which institutions of higher education, through efforts such as moot courts, could try and break down these silos.[21]

Limited project management capacity

Another factor hindering greater involvement of the judiciary in the 2030 Agenda is the limited institutional capacity of the justice sector in project management. Unlike the administrative structures of government departments, the judiciary does not usually have offices dedicated to coordinating project management. This is largely due to the fact that the organizational culture is not generally associated with project design and implementation. The management logic in judicial organizations contrasts sharply with that of the Executive Branch. It is not common to find offices dedicated to management coordination, priority project management, or systematic monitoring of project implementation. Nor is it common to find technological tools for management monitoring and control, such as software and management dashboards, or routine practices for monitoring the progress of management with the departments, such as periodic meetings, publication of information on project implementation, etc.

This limited institutional capacity for public management of the judiciary is also reflected in little progress in incorporating good institutional quality practices into the public sector. The judiciary has not made progress incorporating important recent developments in public management, such as reforms related to government centers. In the executive branch, government centers are the institutions and units that provide direct support to the president, the governor, or the mayor in managing government priorities. Although there are no documented cases in the judicial sector as yet, there is potential to do so. There are also no documented cases

---

[21] See the chapter by Thomas Probert in this volume.

of Supreme Courts or Judicial Councils implementing delivery unit initiatives, which consist of a small team focused on facilitating the achievement of key government priorities.

These tools and institutions are key to advancing public management practices and for adopting project-centered management techniques. They are valuable assets to begin to make judicial institutions more open to consolidated public management practices in the executive branch. These types of reforms can in turn help judiciaries embark upon non-traditional agendas, such as the SDGs and the 2030 Agenda, and to expand its scope of action in the field of sustainable development issues. Again, the role of higher education, and specifically, graduate programs in public administration, have a role to play in advancing the SDGs with a particular focus on increasing the capacity of judicial institutions to at least engage with institutions that are focused on project management.

The lack of monitoring and evaluation

Another challenge for the 2030 Agenda and the SDGs is the absence of capacity to monitor and evaluate justice sector institutions. At the heart of the 2030 Agenda is the definition of sectoral development goals to which public sector institutions commit themselves. This requires, on the one hand, the capacity to define realistic goals based on sound diagnoses and, on the other, the capacity to implement monitoring and evaluation measures that will ultimately make it possible to determine whether the proposed goals have been achieved. However, the judiciary in general lacks dedicated personnel and resources oriented toward monitoring and evaluation. This can be a disincentive to participate in the efforts to adapt to the 2030 Agenda, as it requires planning, monitoring, and evaluation capacities. Pairing judicial institutions or advocating for shadow reporting by graduate students in capstone projects may be one way of addressing this gap.

The lack of evidence-based decision-making culture

In line with limited monitoring and evaluation capacity, judicial institutions also lack internal initiatives that promote the use of evidence in decision-making. This is not in itself an obstacle to greater engagement with the 2030 Agenda and the SDGs, but the existence of such structures would greatly facilitate these types of projects. The ability to generate data, make diagnoses, evaluate results, and adjust the implementation of projects based on empirical evidence would increase the management capacity of the judiciary. This would create better conditions for the judiciary to become more involved and play a more prominent role in global sustainable development agendas. Increasingly, graduate programs in public policy emphasize not only evidence-based decision making but also the use of innovative technologies, such as artificial intelligence and other data platforms for advancing these skills and culture. Such programs also stress the importance for public sector institutions to introduce data governance mechanisms, which are key to unlocking the full potential of data. Justice sector institutions could benefit greatly from these approaches.

Lack of accountability culture

The 2030 Agenda requires a strong accountability component to regularly explain the progress made and, eventually, the obstacles or delays encountered. Setting medium- and long-term goals is not a simple task, and it involves some complexity at the time of implementation. It also involves generating interim information on the various stages of implementation. This exercise of measuring progress must be accompanied by an accountability strategy that allows the population to know the results. The judiciary is often not familiar with this type of practice, has not developed tools or programs to inform the population of the results of its management, and does not have the communications capacity required for this type of action. In addition to technical or institutional limitations, cultural factors also play a role. Often, Supreme Courts and other leading institutions in the justice sector do not feel comfortable with accountability, transparency, and communication mechanisms with the user community and the general public. All of this is an obstacle to encouraging judicial institutions to actively engage in the implementation of the 2030 Agenda. This culture in many ways is out of step with recent advances globally in transparency and accountability discussed below, and in particular, through the Open Government Partnership and similar initiatives. For example, the International Open Justice Network, a regional civil society organization, has been a major advocate in recent years for the introduction of transparency and accountability reforms in Latin American judiciaries.[22] The network has fostered coalitions that have successfully engaged academics and members of higher education institutions in open justice and people-centered reform initiatives, usually framed within the SDGs.

Low citizen participation

As with accountability, the judiciary is generally reluctant to adopt citizen participation tools or practices. This is the result of an institutional culture that for decades, if not centuries, has been characterized by a conception in which judges do not interact with citizens, "speak only through their judgments," have no obligation to be accountable to the population, and use a language full of technical phrases, Latin words, and legal jargon to create a marked distance from the users of the justice system and the population in general.[23] These closed practices and the lack of channels for interaction with the population are an obstacle to the implementation of the 2030 Agenda, as the latter requires interaction with civil society organizations and citizens.[24] It is only since the end of the 20th century that judicial institutions in Latin America and the Caribbean have begun to take steps to change this perception and to see the link with the citizenry as a virtuous opportunity. This shift has led to an opening of the judiciary that, although slow and gradual, allows us to see the beginning of an institutional change that promotes a new vision of the relationship between the courts

---

[22] See for example "Booklet #2. Judicial Transparency Index" (in Spanish), International Open Justice Network, www.redjusticiaabierta.org.
[23] Kevin Lehman, "Proyecto: Problemas y Desafíos de la Comunicación Judicial," Santiago de Chile, Judicial Studies Center of the Americas, 2020.
[24] They also relate to the larger challenges that many in this volume note for the human rights movement overall. See in particular Mendelson's introduction, Andersen's chapter.

and the people. It should be noted that, as with other open justice reforms, schools of law, public affairs, and social sciences have yet to adopt the current standards of institutional quality that could facilitate the advancement of the SDGs within judicial institutions.

Outdated educational paradigms

In Latin America and the Caribbean, justice sector institutions are staffed by professionals who come mostly from law schools, and to a lesser extent from social science, public policy, and public administration. Law schools, in particular, have curricula that are almost exclusively focused on legal issues, ignoring the judicial institution, its characteristics and problems. In other words, there is no focus on the fact that courts are part of complex, bureaucratic and hierarchical organizations, with well-defined processes and products, and are cross-cut by cultural aspects and technological resources. As a result, these graduates lack basic knowledge and tools related to the functioning and challenges of public sector organizations such as justice sector institutions. When they become leaders or members of these institutions, they inevitably have limited approaches, with shortcomings that prevent them from making a leap in institutional quality toward a new paradigm of management of the judiciary, which allows them to assume their responsibilities both with human rights and with sustainable development, inclusive governance, the 2030 Agenda, and the SDGs.

JUDICIAL INSTITUTIONS AND THE SDGs: THE WAY FORWARD

In spite of all the challenges described here, there are many opportunities to help make a quantum leap in engaging the judiciary in the 2030 Agenda and the SDGs. As has been noted, many, if not all of them, involve in some way the next generation and the role of higher education. The following are some scenarios and factors that can be used to design and promote an effective strategy to increase the involvement of judicial institutions in this agenda.

The emergence of the open justice movement

Since the creation of the Open Government Partnership in 2011, a very active community of practice has emerged, particularly in Latin America and the Caribbean, promoting open justice policies. This paradigm consists of the application of tools for citizen participation, transparency, and collaboration in the functioning of judicial institutions. The open justice agenda has several points of contact with the SDGs, particularly SDG 16, which includes among its indicators some directly related to the pillars of open government, such as a significant reduction in corruption (16.5), effective and transparent accountable institutions (16.6), inclusive, participatory, and representative decision-making at all levels that is responsive to needs (16.7), and ensuring public access to information (16.10). In this context, there is a strategic opportunity to link the two agendas, with the expectation that they will mutually reinforce each other and create a catalytic effect that will accelerate reforms, particularly those demanded by the younger generation.

Building and fostering partnerships

Interest in the 2030 Agenda and SDGs is growing in the private sector.[25] The same is true in scientific communities.[26] We see this also

---

[25] For example, in Argentina, in 2017, the Argentine Business Council for Sustainable Development launched an online platform to disseminate business initiatives related to the SDGs. The platform aims to show a multiplicity of voices oriented to the 2030 Agenda. More information available at https://www.ods.ceads.org.ar/. In Colombia, the United Nations Development Program and Business Call to Action, decided to promote synergies and a roadmap to collect and analyze data from the private sector, about its impact and contribution towards the SDGs. For more information, see https://sdgs.un.org/partnerships/private-sector-and-its-contribution-sdgs-journey-data-gathering-through-corporate.

[26] For example, the Global Sustainable Development Report (GSDR) is a United Nations publication prepared by a group of independent scientists aiming to strengthen the science-policy interface at the High-Level Political Forum (HLPF) on Sustainable Development. The report seeks to provide evidence that can help decision-makers accelerate action and overcome impediments that stand in the way of progress on sustainable development. The focus is on accelerating transformation through important entry points and enabling science to support this acceleration. More information available at https://sdgs.un.org/gsdr.

in civil society organizations, in international cooperation, and in the international sustainable development community. At the same time, many of these institutions are interested in the functioning, reform, and modernization of the judiciary, the strengthening of the rule of law, and institutional quality reforms in the justice sector. In this context, there are multiple opportunities to generate partnerships to progressively increase the involvement of the judiciary in the 2030 Agenda, to promote and disseminate the SDGs within the broad set of institutions that make up the justice sector, and to transfer the necessary know-how to strengthen the institutional capacity of these institutions to embark on these types of reforms.

The formation of this type of partnership can help accelerate reforms through actions that contribute to closing the various existing gaps. For example, the knowledge gap must be closed in order to generate materials and practical tools that document different models for addressing the SDGs in the justice sector and provide step-by-step instructions for implementing programs to this end. The statistical and methodological gap must also be closed in order to have inputs and tools for generating data to set targets, to carry out monitoring exercises, and finally, to produce reports based on empirical data. Alliances can be created to articulate the efforts of organizations from different sectors, thus strengthening the communication agenda to highlight achievements and generate incentives for decision-makers in judicial institutions. Universities have a critical role to play in facilitating the development of the skills that form the basis of effective partnerships.

Build on efforts that already exist at the supranational level

In some regions, there are supranational regional institutions related to judicial institutions that have already engaged with the 2030 Agenda and the SDGs, promoting dissemination, awareness, and even implementation actions. In Latin America, for example, the Ibero-American Summit of Supreme Courts, the Central American and Caribbean Judicial Council, and the Conference of Ministers of Justice of Ibero-American Countries stand out.

In addition, international organizations such as UNDP can be extremely important strategic partners. UNDP, in line with its mandate and in close collaboration with colleagues and partners within the UN system and beyond, has taken a leading role in implementing, monitoring, and reporting on peaceful, just, and inclusive societies, and the catalytic role of SDG 16 across the 2030 Agenda. This includes supporting the integration of SDG 16 into national and subnational systems and processes; developing inclusive mechanisms for monitoring, reporting, and accountability for SDG 16 at the national level; generating and disseminating knowledge on the implementation and progress of SDG 16; and building collaborative multi-stakeholder partnerships and linkages to support the achievement of SDG 16. Existing efforts should be leveraged to create synergies in the investment of resources, time, and knowledge.

Partner with national and international nongovernmental organizations including universities

Civil society is key to advancing the 2030 Agenda and the SDGs at the global level. In this regard, there are valuable nongovernmental organizations (NGOs) that are already deeply engaged in this issue. For example, the World Justice Project (WJP) has made tremendous efforts to contribute to the measurement of SDG 16, in particular target 16.3 at the global level.[27] The WJP proposed a new indicator that focuses on people's access to legal aid services or information on civil, rather than criminal, justice issues.[28] In this context, the WJP has conducted surveys of unmet legal needs in dozens of countries to contribute to the measurement of target 16.3. According to the WJP,

> *[...] access to civil justice is necessary for people to redress their grievances, access their rights and entitlements, and for the realization of the broader sustainable development agenda. Without the inclusion of a measurement on access to civil justice, there remains an important gap in*

---

[27] Target 16.3: Promote the rule of law at the national and international levels, and ensure equal access to justice for all.
[28] New proposed Indicator 16.3.3: Proportion of those who experienced a legal problem in the last two years who could access appropriate information or expert help and were able to resolve the problem.

the global monitoring framework for the implementation of the SDGs.[29]

There is a strategic opportunity to build bridges between the efforts of judicial institutions and organizations such as WJP but also, as Andersen, the head of WJP, argues in this volume, with universities. The joint contributions are key to demonstrating the role of justice institutions in achieving the goals of the 2030 Agenda. Working with NGOs and institutions of higher learning can fill gaps and address needs that strengthen and/or complement the efforts of justice sector institutions in implementing the SDGs. In other words, these types of partnerships are key to diversifying data sources for monitoring the progress of the 2030 Agenda by judicial institutions.

Leverage the explosion of social networking

The exponential growth in the use of social networks has created new patterns of interaction both among people and between people and governments. Thus, social networks serve as new channels of communication between public administrations and the population, and particularly younger generations. In this sense, these new technologies have created a wide range of opportunities to increase the effectiveness and speed of interactions that cannot be ignored by justice sector institutions. Across Latin American, Supreme Courts and appellate courts have begun to use platforms such as Instagram, X and YouTube on a daily basis to communicate with their users and the population in general, reaching younger generations in novel ways.[30] This has also been the case for international courts such as the Inter-American Court of Human Rights.

---

[29] See Andersen chapter in this volume. See also WJP, no date, "16.3.3 Indicator Proposal Access to Civil Justice", available at https://worldjusticeproject.org/our-work/publications/working-papers/access-civil-justice-indicator-proposal-sdg-target-1633.

[30] See Alvaro Herrero and Ines Selvood "Open Justice and communication: Can social networks close the feedback loop?" in *Towards a Global Open Justice Agenda: Experiences from Latin America*, eds. A. Herrero, I. Selvood and M. Heller (Editorial Jusbaires, 2020), 293–322.

Social networks can be a key tool for designing new, promising strategies that allow for better accountability of judicial institutions and innovative actions to increase citizen participation. All this would allow the judiciary to highlight its initiatives and commitments around the 2030 Agenda, spreading the social value and public impact of the goals adopted.

CONCLUSION

The judiciary across Latin America and the Caribbean still has enormous potential to strengthen its interest in, and commitment to, the 2030 Agenda and the SDGs. This chapter has highlighted the progress made so far, as well as the obstacles and opportunities to continue on the path toward sustainable and inclusive development that leaves no one behind. It has also provided some suggestions to support the efforts of judicial institutions in this regard and highlighted the existence of an ecosystem of judicial, governmental, and civil society actors that can be better harnessed to strengthen the implementation of the 2030 Agenda.

There is a premise underlying this chapter that deserves to be made explicit. Judicial institutions are different than they were a century ago. They are not simply impartial actors in the resolution of controversies between different actors in society. On the contrary, they are institutions that have evolved considerably, undergoing radical changes and significantly expanding their scope of action. In addition to the classic figures of judges, prosecutors, and public defenders specializing in gender, housing, and children's issues, they have gradually been joined by sophisticated offices for legal advice and counseling, alternative dispute resolution, and centers for vulnerable groups. The judicial sector is no longer a passive actor, receiving conflicts to be resolved, but is proactively implementing policies to, for example, improve access to justice, reduce gender inequality, and increase environmental protection.

Therefore, when it comes to the SDGs, the judiciary can no longer remain neutral or indifferent. Judicial institutions play an extremely important role in political systems, with relevant implications for various aspects of the functioning of our societies, such as the protection of fundamental rights, the prevention of violence, the maintenance of harmonious social coexistence, the inclusion of disadvantaged groups, the defense of collective rights, and the control of abuses of power by political, economic, and social actors. In such a context, it seems inevitable that the judiciary should begin a transition from a role of passive platform for conflict resolution to one of strong leadership, commensurate with its institutional responsibilities. This will not only contribute significantly to the advancement of the SDGs but will also improve the public perception of the institutional authority of the judiciary.

Efforts of judicial institutions to adapt and implement the 2030 Agenda should not be limited to SDG 16 but ought to adopt a broader and more ambitious approach in line with the "new profile" of the judiciary in our societies. In other words, the judiciary is in a position to set targets related to the 17 SDGs, including issues such as gender, poverty, inequality, environment, climate change, and renewable energy. This approach would reflect a more realistic and appropriate conception of the breadth of its institutional role, more typical of a branch of government than of a mere conflict resolution body, and in line with the interests of future generations.

However, this will not be possible without the engagement of higher education institutions. The preceding sections have highlighted the multiple opportunities for law schools, public policy, and related disciplines to become catalysts for a paradigm shift to bring new approaches and tools to justice institutions. Universities are poised to play a central role in the cultural transformation of the justice sector in Latin America and the Caribbean which in turn will contribute to the advancement of the SDGs and the 2030 Agenda.

Finally, it should be emphasized that a broader and more ambitious approach to the 2030 Agenda also implies a greater commitment to human rights and fundamental freedoms on the part of judicial institutions. The SDGs as a whole reflect a broad constellation of human rights recognized in various international treaties, including fundamentally, socioeconomic ones. If the judiciary engages more deeply with the 2030 Agenda, it will also be committing itself to a new way of protecting fundamental human rights, which is at the core of its institutional mission in the constitutional system.

4

THE POTENTIAL OF PARTICIPATORY AND EXPERIENTIAL LEARNING FOR THE PROMOTION OF HUMAN RIGHTS AND THE SDGs

Thomas Probert

University of Pretoria, South Africa & University of Cambridge, UK

ABSTRACT

This chapter will consider two experiential learning techniques drawn from human rights education – mooting and shadow reporting – and consider how they might inform initiatives to increase awareness of and participation in the work of the SDGs. It proposes a simulacre reporting exercise as a means of having students engage with the global indicator framework, national and local official data, relevant consultation or observation, and prevailing policy frameworks. This report, that could be drafted as part of a class or clinical group exercise, would enhance data literacy, data analytics, and data-presentation skills but would also encourage students to place normative frameworks in the context of the lived experience of their local communities.

Keywords: Experiential learning; localization; shadow reporting; data; SDG indicators

> *"One could hardly think of a better way to advance the cause of human rights than to bring together students, who are the leaders, judges and teachers of tomorrow ... to debate some of the crucial issues of our time in the exciting and challenging atmosphere of a courtroom, where they can test their arguments and skills against one another in the spirit of fierce but friendly competition."*
>
> Nelson Mandela, welcoming participants to the 1995 African Human Rights Moot Court Competition[1]

BACKGROUND

The concept of "SDG 16+" draws upon an emphasis on interlinkages and co-dependencies between different parts of the Sustainable Development Goals (SDGs) and brings together the core governance and safety concerns of SDG 16 with those other targets that play a vital role in undergirding such development.[2] Among them is Target 4.7 on – among other things – human rights education. Target 4.7 aims to ensure that by 2030

> all learners acquire knowledge and skills needed to promote sustainable development, including among others through education for sustainable development and sustainable lifestyles, human rights, gender equality, promotion of a culture of peace and non-violence, global citizenship, and appreciation of cultural diversity and of culture's contribution to sustainable development.[3]

Making the connection between human rights education (alongside other pro-developmental and conscious global citizenship education) and the broader SDG 16+ agenda also has implications

---

[1] Quoted in Gift Kgomosotho, Christof Heyns, and Bongani Majola, "Notes from the Field: Bringing New Life to Human Rights Globally: The Powerful Tool of Schools' Moots," *International Journal of Human Rights Education* 2, no. 1 (2018): 1.
[2] SDG16+ is a concept often associated with the Pathfinders initiative, a group of UN member countries, international organizations, and members of civil and the private sector, see https://www.sdg16.plus.
[3] See https://sdgs.un.org/goals/goal4.

for the creation of meaningful *partnerships* for the Goals. Agenda 2030 will not work as an elite-driven top-down exercise in or from New York. It has often been highlighted that one of the advantages of the SDGs over the MDGs is their universality. A corollary of this is the importance of the activation of a "cohort 2030" *across the world*.[4]

The activation of such a cohort will directly contribute toward another vital quality necessary to make the Agenda as a whole function, namely *accountability*. The framework was designed partly to act as a peer-reviewed network of State-level exchange (via fora such as the High-Level Political Forum), but to be effective there must also be a meaningful level of ground-up participatory reflexion. Without education for the general population about the SDGs, this reflexion will only ever be partial.

Thus far, a great deal of sensitization and awareness-raising around the SDGs has been about *branding*. The SDGs have undoubtedly been well-branded, and the cubes and colors have to a certain extent achieved recognition. However, at that level, they will always remain aspirational rather than practical, and organizational rather than operational. The public pursuit of accountability to aspirational objectives will always be inherently political, and though some may argue this is a strength – it is possible, after all, that a politics of generality can empower a more technical process of review – its promises may prove empty, and its energy could easily be misdirected, without capacity at local levels to engage with the technical policy implications.

Therefore, this education regarding the SDGs needs to extend beyond the modification and updating of syllabi within development studies, political science, or international law programmes. Something further is needed to have learners *experience* the ways in which the SDGs can shape policymaking at local, regional, or national levels.

---

[4] On Cohort 2030, see Sarah Mendelson, "Young People, the Sustainable Development Goals, and the Liberal World Order: What is to be done?" *Medium*, October 9, 2018, https://medium.com/sdg16plus/young-people-the-sustainable-development-goals-and-the-liberal-world-order-what-is-to-be-done-fc648e3b2d21.

TWO EXAMPLES FROM HUMAN RIGHTS EDUCATION

Human rights practitioners will recognize this two-level operation: the way in which the rhetorical deployment of the language of human rights can be divorced from the more mechanical operation of the "work" of human rights protection.

Here, I want to learn from two techniques developed and used within (mainly legal) human rights education as a means of sensitizing while developing both knowledge and skills, at different levels: namely the facilitation of *human rights moots* and the production of *human rights shadow reports*. At least at the university level (and I shall discuss below how at least the moot can and has been deployed with younger learners), these techniques build upon a conviction that the next generation of practitioners will only truly understand the mechanics of human rights law through their use. Participatory and experiential learning offer the potential for transformative engagement both with detail and with purpose.

It is worth noting that at the outset of the African Moot, which imagined a court before which the human rights questions of the continent could be litigated, the African Court of Human and Peoples' Rights did not yet exist! The dynamic energy created around the prospect and purpose of such an institution was planted in the fertile minds of a generation of law students, who have gone on to become the current cohorts of human rights professionals (and other lawyers) across the continent. Many of them are working in the context where access to justice in front of the Arusha Court is still a remote possibility.[5]

The practicalities of conducting a moot are quite simple: a problem is designed, usually involving a fictitious State (or group

---

[5] While the Court was created when 15 States ratified the 1998 Protocol in 2004 (more than twenty years after the first African Moot), direct access to the Court for individuals is limited to matters arising in the jurisdiction of States that have also made Article 34(6) declarations – that is currently only 8 (12 having been made, with 4 having been subsequently withdrawn). See further Frans Viljoen, Keketso Kgomosotho, Thompson Chengeta, and Nyambeni Davhana, "Christof and mooting," in *A Life Interrupted: Essays in Honour of the Lives and Legacies of Christof Heyns,* eds. Frans Viljoen et al. (PULP, 2022), 86.

of States, to introduce more complex, public international law questions), and a set of established facts. A litigating posture is then envisioned with an applicant alleging violation of several human rights, and the State, as respondent, disputing the extent to which their conduct violates provisions of the instrument in question (in the case of the African Moot, the African Charter on Human and Peoples' Rights). Teams are invited to draft written briefs for both of the two parties, and then based on the written submissions, a certain number of teams (in the case of the African Moot, one per country) are invited to the oral arguments.

Moots bring multiple benefits for law students: in addition to the obvious skills development with respect to problem analysis, issue-finding, and research, the written memorials are an opportunity to showcase drafting and argumentation skills. For those teams selected for oral presentation, there are clear opportunities to practise oral presentation and time management. More normatively, well-designed problems or cases allow students to explore the integration and synthesis between different branches of international law.[6] Likewise, the problem can allow for the important inclusion of topics or populations, spotlighting issues that receive insufficient attention within conventional legal education in particular contexts (minority rights being an obvious example).

These benefits for the development of the advocacy skills of law students have made moots a staple of legal education for centuries. More recently moots focussed on certain areas of law, especially international law, have been developed as a means of encouraging attention and excitement around the possibility for the use of those areas of law, and opportunities for future careers. From the perspective of a global campus for human rights, the competition between teams from the global north and the global south, or across other diverse demographics, can make a strong contribution

---

[6] This discussion draws upon Christof Heyns, Norman Taku, and Frans Viljoen, "Revolutionising Human Rights Education in African Universities the African Human Rights Moot Court Competition," in *Advocating for Human Rights: 10 Years of the Inter-American Moot Court Competition*, eds. Claudio Grossman, Claudia Martin, and Diego Rodríguez-Pinzón (Martinus Nijhoff, 2008).

toward universalism. The pride of a team from an African university winning a world moot competition in which teams from elite Western universities were also competing cannot be overestimated.[7]

But there is also a less-advanced, mass-popular version – the National Schools Moot – which is not intended necessarily to guide the next generation of lawyers but rather the next generation of citizens (and – indeed – indirectly, some of the older generations too). Less tied to an international human rights instrument, this model can be a more local exercise in constitutional awareness, where a rights-issue articulated in the SDGs can be argued with reference to the rights articulated in the domestic constitution. As such it can form a core part of a civics education curriculum for learners of any age. One theory of change here is that the activity not only has an impact on the learners themselves, but also upon family members and others with whom they discuss activities from their school day.

Such a device for suffusing an awareness of the SDGs, the "future we want," and the legitimate expectations of the public concerning the steps taken by their governments to achieve them could be transformational.

However, a potential complication arises given the obvious significance of a confrontational or adversarial dimension of a legal proceeding for how the role-play of a moot court works. It is sometimes contended that one of the significant merits of the SDGs over conventional human rights frameworks, for those looking to advance justice and governance objectives, is that they represent a less-confrontational framing for important questions of rights. As such, therefore, it is difficult to conceive how one could create an "SDG moot" with an applicant and respondent.

Indeed, this challenge is in ways symptomatic of a broader concern about how human rights practitioners should leverage the SDGs: if the aspirations laid out in Agenda 2030 are treated like other rights documents, and passivity on the part of the State is

---

[7] A South African university first won the Jessup International Law Moot Court Competition in 1999; the Nelson Mandela World Human Rights Moot Competition (which began in 2009) has been won by teams from Jamaica, Brazil, Argentina, and Kenya.

responded to using the same grammar as in human rights politics, then an important opportunity to renew the agenda of justice may be missed. But at the same time, as discussed above, if the SDGs are allowed to remain aspirational rhetoric, rather than applied policy to confront demonstrated problems, then increasing awareness and literacy of them will be a hollow victory.

This highlights the significance of another potential benefit or consequence of a human rights moot that Christof Heyns and others have recognized. The design of the problems, and the fact that participants must prepare both sides of the case, lead to an outcome they described as "placing positivism in context."[8] Where legal rules meet real-world conditions, operative policy consideration ("lesser of two evils") or principles of fairness may impact the interpretation of positivistic rules. Just as lawyers must learn to place rules alongside priorities, such as cost-effectiveness, development practitioners must wrestle with the interplay between internationally declared objectives and governmental realities such as sticky bureaucracies or the independence of magistrates and judges. They must also comprehend how policy choices are shaped by, for example, the collection of priorities or the lack of investment in data-processing within government records.

In addition to mooting, one can add another example of a participatory and experiential exercise from human rights education, namely the classwork of *shadow reporting*. This is usually undertaken by clinical groups in a law school setting (rather than as an individual assignment) and can involve direct engagement with both international mechanisms and individual rights-holders.

From a pedagogical perspective, this exercise seems more useful for getting into the detail of a particular issue or context, and maybe less useful for sensitizing a class to the mechanics of a wider process, and it relies upon a much higher baseline level of knowledge. But it still introduces important dimensions of the system to which it contributes (usually UN or regional reporting processes): starting, simply, with the fact that the process is going

---

[8] Heyns, Taku, and Viljoen, "Revolutionising Human Rights Education," 20–21.

on, that the State in question has participated; at a more granular level, allowing exploration of the issues at question and what the State has said about itself.

Unlike mooting, shadow reporting does not involve role play but can still involve adversariality that can so contribute toward participatory learning by way of its critical perspective toward the State's official position. This requires students to test the assumptions of the narrative presented in the State's representation, to whatever treaty body, and to research a particular issue, or potentially a wide range of issues, using both official and unofficial data. An effective shadow report will both contextualize and augment. The process of writing it will involve challenging the veracity of objective claims made by the government and discussing the fairness of subjective assessments presented. This lays the groundwork for public accountability with respect to the implementation of national or other development agendas.

Meanwhile, like a well-designed moot problem, shadow reports can be used to cast a spotlight on subjects which are receiving insufficient attention elsewhere within a curriculum, or within national policy debates. The whole point is to add a perspective to the reading of the main report, often on behalf of a minority group whose interests have not been sufficiently included. In this respect, shadow reports that give a voice to otherwise ignored communities can strongly reinforce the SDG principle of "leave no one behind." Importantly, rather than the fictional fact-pattern of mooting, in this case, students work with real issues, sometimes on behalf of actual clients. Engaging with these clients, directly learning the way in which existing policy may be excluding or marginalizing them is an important alternate way of "placing positivism in context." These opportunities for consultation with, or at least close empirical observation of, affected communities can be some of the most enriching experiences of clinical legal studies.

These engagements can turn shadow reporting into fully participatory learning, but even without them, the process of producing such a report will be a more engaged form of assignment than a typical essay. It is also worth underlining that, alongside their pedagogical benefits, the products of this process, the shadow reports themselves, often play a vital role in facilitating the work of international organizations, and as entry-points for constructive dialogue with governmental stakeholders at national level.[9]

Shadow reports can make a vital contribution to the way in which treaty bodies undertake meaningful reviews of State practice. Depending upon the character of the mechanism to which they are submitted, they can also be the basis for direct engagement with officials for students themselves.[10] At the very least, they provide the sense of making a contribution to a real-world process, and the sense of satisfaction when a pertinent question is asked of a State representative on the basis of research that had been contributed to the Secretariat by way of a shadow report. Neither experience should be underestimated. Likewise, shadow reports provide a mechanism for students effectively to advocate for real-world clients in front of real-world mechanisms, allowing them to appreciate the responsibility of representation as well as to tackle substantive issues.

THE PROPOSAL: A SHADOW OR SIMULACRE SDG REPORT DRAFTING PROCESS

The contribution here, then, is the proposal of an exercise for role-played participatory reporting – fusing the benefits of mooting and shadow reporting into a single exercise that can contribute toward a more sophisticated understanding of the operationalization of the SDGs, rather than just the branding.

---

[9] See, for example, Joel Pruce, "The Ferguson Uprising, Shadow Reporting, and Human Rights Experimentalism," *Human Rights Quarterly* 45 (2023): 88–108. See also Eric Tars, "Human Rights Shadow Reporting: A Strategic Tool for Domestic Justice," *Journal of Poverty Law and Policy* 42 (2009): 475–85.

[10] An increasing array of international human rights actors, both intergovernmental and nongovernmental, are leveraging the enthusiasm of law clinics to assist in the mechanics of State review. This kind of involvement for students is of course a tremendous opportunity, but it extends a little beyond the remit of what could be considered shadow reporting.

This exercise could be run with senior schoolchildren (maybe 16–18 years) as well as with university students in a politics, governance, or human rights class. In order to make it a manageable classroom exercise, and for the reasons discussed above related to the overlap with human rights education, SDG 16+ should be an explicit framing.[11]

In cases where the State in question has recently produced a Voluntary National Report (VNR) or another form of an SDG Report (SDGR), it may make sense for this exercise to produce a genuine shadow report, one that engages directly with the real product. Given the participatory and inclusive way in which States are encouraged to produce VNRs, there may well be official opportunities to engage with the process. At present, the international consideration of VNRs (such as there is one) does not provide a forum for the discussion or strategic publication of shadow reports, but again, opportunities might be sought nationally.

Alternatively, given the proliferation of Voluntary *Local* Reviews (VLRs), another possibility would be for universities to engage with local authorities in their city or municipality in order to contribute toward the drafting of some kind of comprehensive local review.[12] As noted, these can be an opportunity to highlight the interests of a particular community, as part of "leaving no one behind."[13]

In other circumstances, though, it is proposed that this could be an entirely simulacre report writing process, at the national level.

---

[11] Within the SDG16+ agenda, there is a wide array of different material to cover, and educators may feel that a further narrowing of scope is appropriate, perhaps selecting 10 indicators for students to choose between.

[12] For an interesting review of the state of VLRs, see Fernanda Ortiz-Moya, Zhonghan Tan, and Yatsuka Katoaka, *State of the Voluntary Local Reviews 2023: Follow-Up and Review of the 2030 Agenda at the Local Level* (IGES, July 2020), https://www.iges.or.jp/en/pub/vlrs-2023/en.

[13] See, for example, the SDG Audit of Black Communities in Kansas City, Missouri conducted as a capstone project at the Columbia University School of International and Public Affairs, https://www.sipa.columbia.edu/sites/default/files/2024-06/For_Publication_KansasCityTaskForce_Mann%20%282%29.pdf.

What Should Such a Report Include?

This chapter is not the space for a detailed discussion of what actual VNRs or SDGRs ought to look like (indeed, not even to suggest that there is a singular model), but it is worth dwelling on what might be encouraged for inclusion within a shadow report so as to create the richest engagement for the students with the full range of the SDGs.

The students should be guided in how to find, verify, present, and discuss the various types of data. They should explore which policy-making organs are likely to have the greatest role to play with respect to each of the many issues potentially raised by the target and indicator framework. Finally, especially for more advanced students, they ought to explore how peer-reviewed or other research from the academy or other sources might inform or critique government policies that have been adopted.

Data

There should be detailed engagement with the agreed international indicator framework, including reference to the feasibility of collection and presentation of the relevant data based on official statistics. This data aspect is an element of the SDGs that often gets overlooked in introductory texts and is considered too technical. This tendency is a serious misstep, and certainly, at the university level, an underestimation of the capacity and potential of students. However, when presenting the exercise, it is worth bearing in mind that the teacher or lecturer may need to dwell on how these indicators interact with the relevant targets, rather than relying on the students' background reading. Moreover, in the event that an official statistic is not available, or an available official statistic only partially captures the scope of the indicator, then they should engage in a discussion of localization (or domestication) and the use of proxy indicators.

Domestication, and especially a normative assessment of the appropriateness of domestication in specific cases, seems likely to be a non-intuitive concept to students who are not well-grounded in empirical social science research, or who are not familiar with the mechanics of official statistical organizations. This presents an opportunity to increase students' awareness of such mechanics and the agencies involved (and in certain cases, potentially the opportunity for engagement with such agencies).[14]

Students should also be introduced to the principle of disaggregation. This has become a buzzword for the SDG community in a way that has arguably been slightly overwrought.[15] Statistical confidence is surely the first hurdle and while, for administrative data, the capacity to disaggregate is merely a function of granular collection, for some of the other (and some or the most important and least well-covered indicators) survey-based data, the "lift" required to get results that can be disaggregated becomes a lot heavier. However, the principled normative reason for the emphasis on disaggregation where possible is an important means of unpacking what it really means to "leave no one behind."

One part of disaggregation that may be accessible, and which may appeal to a student group, would be localization. In contexts that are more data-rich, universities may wish to consider a simulacre VLR rather than a simulacre VNR, regardless of whether, as noted, they are formally collaborating with local authorities.[16] In circumstances

---

[14] For example, with respect to SDG Indicator 16.1.4, which concerns perceptions of safety, but in many cases has been adapted to local conditions. Students might be invited to discuss the merits of using survey data about perceptions of safety collected only from heads of households, or a survey question that has only asked about how safe a respondent feels walking in their local neighborhood rather than one that doesn't specify "local neighbourhood" but does specify "at night."

[15] For a range of commentary on approaches to disaggregation and its significance for the SDGs, see the reports of the Inter-Agency and Expert Group on SDG Indicators, https://unstats.un.org/sdgs/iaeg-sdgs/disaggregation/#:~:text=Data%20Disaggregation%20for%20the%20SDG,of%20leaving%20no%20one%20behind.

[16] In the UK, for example, a research institute at the University of Bristol partnered with local city authorities and an Alliance of other stakeholders to produce the UK's first Voluntary Local Review in 2019. See *Bristol and the SDGs: A Voluntary Local Review of Progress 2019* (2019), https://www.bristol.ac.uk/media-library/sites/cabot-institute-2018/documents/BRISTOL%20AND%20THE%20SDGS.pdf. In the acknowledgments of that report, the authors highlight informative contributions made by

where it is not possible to reinforce an official local process, the university should still consider having the students design some form of public consultation as part of their writing process.

In many contexts, the students will be frustrated in their search for official data about large proportions of the indicator framework. This frustration is worth exploring from a normative perspective (including in the context of SDG Target 17.19 focused on measurements of progress by 2030) but also creates a learning opportunity with respect to the way approximations might be inferred from imperfect or over-specific, non-official sources of data. There should also be opportunities to evidence a report with more narrative data, telling stories about the impact of policies, or about the persistence of challenges, by drawing upon observational research or consultation.

Having been introduced to the official indicator framework and encouraged deeply to research specific parts of the SDG 16+ agenda, it is likely that students will want to propose a number of additional indicators. This could be a valuable part of the exercise, and an opportunity to explore the policy equities involved, and the potential process for making such a proposal.

Policy

Perhaps the greatest difference between a typical shadow report and the proposed simulacre exercise lies with respect to the applicable policy environment. Whereas a shadow report would assume that the case for existing policy has already been expressed, and rather focus on its shortfalls, and make the case for reforms, in the simulacre exercise the students are encouraged to be carrying the government pen, making the case for the progress that has been made, now more than half-way through the lifespan of the SDGs.

The report would fundamentally be asking: what are the policies and programmes that contribute most directly to the achievement of these targets? Depending on the structure of the State (for example, whether there is a centralized planning department, or a

---

other cities and municipalities: Los Angeles and New York in the US, and Santana de Parnaíba in Brazil.

national development plan), this research may look quite different, but in most cases, it will involve developing a granular knowledge of how high-level policy goals are translated into administrative action.

Of course, where students have been able to engage with a prior VNR, or even a baseline report, then such a policy review can focus on more recent policy innovations. Where these reports have not been written, then a more holistic analysis may be appropriate. In addition to presenting the intention of the policy, however, depending on the data revealed, the report may also need to include a realistic analysis of the challenges faced in the implementation of these programmes.

Applied Research

The inclusion of applied research, especially peer-reviewed technical research is probably more appropriate in the case of university-level students (though advanced school-age students could be introduced to curated examples). This could be a particularly interesting part of the exercise for multi-disciplinary human rights classes, or for other groups with a diversity of academic backgrounds. There is also the potential for students at a more advanced level to consider the design of their own research with the indicator framework in mind, or for a linkage to be designed between this reporting exercise and further research of the clinical group.

Again, there would be a subtle distinction between the shadow and simulacre versions – whereas the former can adopt an advocacy stance of "this seems to work; why is the State not doing it?" while the latter – in circumstances where State policy is unresponsive to available evidence – is harder to draft. As discussed in the next section, one device to assist here would be the role-play of consultants, creating a little space between the author and the responsible government ministry.

The Possibility of Role-Play

Acknowledging the reality of the way in which many States go about drafting their VNRs or SDGRs, one way of presenting this exercise to a class would be to envision a contract as consultants, rather than government actors themselves.[17] This would allow the teacher to act as the government agency contracting the service, the client, and can create potentially helpful learning moments.

Alternatively – or additionally – classes could create a simulacre of the kind of intra-ministerial drafting teams that many States use to ensure widespread contributions to their SDG reporting. Small teams could act as representatives from those governmental departments whose work is most implicated by the targets included among SDG 16+ (Justice, Police, Correctional Services, Social Development, Home Affairs, Education, etc.). Another team, representing the consultants, could then canvass these departments for briefings on the relevant policies.

These "report drafting committees" would likely be a venue for interesting role play in contexts where States have already engaged in some way with the SDG process – creating an opportunity for an overlap between simulacre and shadow drafting. Where the prior engagement has shortcomings – for example, where a questionable decision has been taken with respect to domestication, where relevant data has been excluded from reporting, where policies have (in the view of the class) been mis-represented – then the teacher could role-play a scenario where the "consultants" make representations to their "client" about a revised approach in the "upcoming" report.

THE POTENTIAL

Just as with the clinical techniques from human rights education discussed here, the proposed exercise seems likely to have several pedagogical upsides. The exercise provides an opportunity for a detailed investigation of various problem areas addressed by the SDG 16+ agenda, the design of the various targets, the utility of the indicator framework for measuring them. Beyond this, the exercise

---

[17] The exercise could be run as either an individual or group-based exercise. The possibility for role-play is perhaps greater as a group exercise, but some preambular individual preparation would likely add value.

will require a qualitative and deeply contextualized assessment of the extent to which that developmental challenge is experienced in the given context, or how the marginalization of certain groups may exacerbate it. Moreover, the exercise can provide an informative lesson about the current state of the problem (coupled with data literacy skills, data analytics, and data-presentation). It will introduce the current state of government policy directed toward the problem area, which could involve a political assessment of motives and values. It should involve consultation with affected groups, or at least close observation of their lived experiences. Finally, it will offer an opportunity for a potentially detailed literature review of the "pracademic" literature on "what works?"

More broadly, of course, the central thrust of the exercise is to lead to greater ownership of the SDGs, both in their aspiration and purpose, but also in the practice of development, and of the instrumentality of the indicator framework. Both this knowledge and experience can play a foundational role in gestating and growing "cohort 2030."[18]

In considering this broad potential significance, it seems worth weighing the merit of the emphasis on the data and the government processes (the simulacre report) over the advocacy for greater attention paid to "what works" and (nongovernmental) development programming (more akin to the shadow report). Put differently, why is it significant that students become aware of and engaged with the mechanics of the SDGs in addition to the purposes and objectives?

This is not a binary option: especially for younger learners, it is important that the promise of "what works?" or "what can work?" is centered as well as questions such as "is there political will to achieve this?" But, especially now, during the second half of the lifespan of the SDGs, it seems important to focus on questions of review and, to return to the theme introduced at the outset, *accountability*.

---

[18] Mendelson, "Young People, the Sustainable Development Goals, and the Liberal World Order." See also Sarah E. Mendelson, "Building the Field of Sustainable Development," *Stanford Social Innovation Review*, Winter 2020, https://ssir.org/articles/entry/f oundations_should_invest_in_building_the_field_of_ sustainable_development.

The set of questions this entails – (i) to what extent is a goal being advanced by existing policy? (ii) are there particular groups who are being left behind? (iii) what can be done to catch up? – could be one of most transformative impacts of a human rights-based approach upon the work of the SDGs. For learners, these are not questions that can be encouraged without creating opportunities to engage with the targets of SDG 16+ in a more instrumental and data-driven way. Exercises such as the one proposed here, whether simulacre or connected with material assistance to official processes, can help achieve this outcome.

5

TOWARD MORE JUST SOCIETIES: THE SDG AGENDA AND INNOVATIONS IN HIGHER EDUCATION

Ariel C. Armony

Babson College, USA

ABSTRACT

This chapter delves into the significant role Higher Education Institutions (HEIs) play in advancing the Sustainable Development Goals (SDGs) aim of strengthening and refocusing institutional efforts toward the 2030 Agenda and beyond. Acknowledging the limited progress made toward the 2030 Agenda, the chapter discusses the extent to which universities are meeting their social and ethical responsibilities in fostering sustainable development and human rights. Through an examination of the relationship between universities and the SDGs (including criticism of their role in reinforcing urban inequalities), the chapter articulates a vision for HEIs to embrace transformative partnerships, interdisciplinary approaches, and community engagement to rebuild public trust and reinforce their place as pivotal actors in driving social and economic progress. Three essential tasks for HEIs are identified: fostering SDG synergies, establishing trust and collaboration with local communities, and advancing a data-informed progress assessment that provides a roadmap for how to use the SDGs to further new agendas.

Keywords: Higher education institutions; social justice; human rights; SDG 16; rankings; 2030 Agenda

"We do not need more warnings. The dystopian future is already here." With these words, the United Nations (UN) High Commissioner for Human Rights Volker Türk set the stage for an appraisal of the 2030 Agenda for Sustainable Development. As Türk told delegates at the Human Rights Council in Geneva on September 11, 2023, "we are on target for [the 2030 Agenda] to become a tragic monument to the failure of our generation to erase extreme poverty and realize human rights."[1] Former UN Secretary-General Ban Ki-moon's promise that the 2015 adoption of the Sustainable Development Goals (SDGs) would be "a defining moment in human history" has gone largely unrealized, with many arguing that the world is further from the sustainable development achievements now than it was nearly a decade ago. In fact, a UN progress report acknowledged that "progress on more than 50 percent of targets of the SDGs is weak and insufficient; on 30 percent, it has stalled or gone into reverse."[2] This disappointing trajectory has led many to question whether institutional leaders worldwide are truly committed to realizing the promise of SDGs. *New York Times* columnist Nicholas Kristof went so far as to describe the 2023 UN General Assembly in New York as a combination of "Cocktails, Steak, and Hypocrisy."[3] This frustration was echoed by the many

---

[1] Volker Türk, "Türk: Human rights are antidote to prevailing politics of distraction, deception, indifference and repression," *United Nations Human Rights*, September 11, 2023, https://www.ohchr.org/en/statements/2023/09/turk-human-rights-are-antidote-prevailing-politics-distraction-deception.
[2] United Nations, "The Sustainable Development Goals Report Special Edition," 2023, https://unstats.un.org/sdgs/report/2023/The-Sustainable-Development-Goals-Report-2023.pdf.
[3] Nicholas Kristof, "Coming Soon in New York: Cocktails, Steak and Hypocrisy," *The New York Times*, September 16, 2023, https://www.nytimes.com/2023/09/16/opinion/un-sustainability-goals-poverty.html?smid=nytcore-ios-share&referringSource=articleShare.

protestors who gathered around Times Square in New York at the start of Climate Week in September 2023, calling for the US government to act on climate change and stop fossil fuel dependency. The signs they carried expressed angst and rage: "We can't work in a wildfire," "Climate S.O.S," and "Stop Co_2lonialism."[4]

If the 2030 Agenda is unrealistic or already a failure, what is the purpose of adhering to the SDGs? By reaffirming this agenda, and even committing more resources to it, are we as institutional leaders complicit in the hypocrisy Kristof described? The purpose of this chapter is not to settle these questions, but to reflect on the SDGs' aim of strengthening and refocusing our institutional efforts toward the 2030 Agenda and beyond. I will center on Higher Education Institutions (HEI) specifically in the United States and consider some lessons that hold promise but require immediate, focused, and sustained action from universities. With this, I will also highlight some specific and actionable strategies that HEIs can take on to better facilitate the SDG agenda. As I will detail below, universities are uniquely positioned to support the ideals of the SDGs, and achieving these goals can measurably improve public confidence in universities as well as enhance the university experience for students, faculty, staff, and communities alike. My discussion will highlight SDG 16: Peace, Justice, and Strong Institutions.

WHY UNIVERSITIES?

The literature on the connection between universities and the SDG agenda is abundant. A search across sources using the keywords "SDG" and "HEI" on Google Scholar returned 7,290 articles since 2015. In addition to possessing extensive research capabilities, many universities are also home to centers and institutes that facilitate the cross-fertilization of ideas. With these resources, HEIs facilitate the exchange of knowledge, ideas, experiences, and best

---

[4] Reuters, "Climate Protesters in New York Send Message to United Nations," September 18, 2023, https://www.reuters.com/pictures/climate-protesters-new-york-send-message-united-nations-2023-09-18/.

practices that help shape cross-cultural understanding and collaboration through partnerships within and across nations. Partnerships play a vital role in harnessing the full potential of universities in advancing the SDG agenda by bridging local and global engagement. Collaborations among universities, governments, businesses, and civil society organizations can amplify the impact of sustainable initiatives, leverage resources, and contribute to scaling solutions. Universities serve as key conveners for smart investment in their cities and regions, act as engines for knowledge production, and train new generations of practitioners.[5]

Universities' decisions have significant implications for their communities. Some institutions have adopted Carnegie Mellon University's model of the Voluntary University Review (VUR).[6] In the process, universities have learned not only about the hard work of tracking and reporting their engagement with the SDGs but also the challenges involved in accelerating actions and sustaining institutional commitment.[7]

The world communicates about the SDGs through voluntary reporting. Designed initially at the state level, the process (and product) has evolved to include cities and regions conducting Voluntary Local Reviews. In 2020, Carnegie Mellon adapted the process to the university setting through a first Voluntary University

---

[5] Sustainable Development Solutions Network, "Accelerating Education for the SDGs in Universities: A Guide for Universities, Colleges, and Tertiary and Higher Education Institutions," September 2020, https://irp-cdn.multiscreensite.com/be6d1d56/files/uploaded/accelerating-education-for-the-sdgs-in-unis-web_zZuYLaoZRHK1L77zAd4n.pdf.

[6] Carnegie Mellon University Sustainability Initiative, "2020 Voluntary University Review of the Sustainable Development Goals," Carnegie Mellon University, 2020, https://www.cmu.edu/sustainability-initiative/review/cmu-vur-2020.pdf.

[7] Ángel Cabrera and Drew Cutright, *Higher Education and SDG17: Partnerships for the Goals*. (Emerald Publishing, 2023); Nikhil Seth, "SDG 17 and the Role of Universities Achieving Agenda 2030," in *Higher Education and SDG17: Partnerships for the Goals*, eds. Ángel Cabrera and Drew Cutright (Emerald Publishing, 2023), 19–25; Duncan Ross. "Higher Education's Role in Advancing the SDGs in the G20: Progress & Opportunities," *Times Higher Education*, August 2023, https://www.timeshighereducation.com/sites/default/files/g20_report.pdf.

Review (VUR) to assess how CMU's education, research, and practice aligned with the SDGs. As CMU provost Jim Garrett wrote in the introduction to that first VUR,

> *Our intention is for CMU's VUR to be a framework for us to track what we are doing across the 17 Global Goals and where we might find opportunities to do more. We also hope that by issuing this VUR, we will spark action at other institutions of higher education to do the same.*[8]

Can universities make a difference concerning SDG implementation? In the introduction to their book on Higher Education and SDG 17, Ángel Cabrera and Drew Cutright argue that universities' engagement with the 2030 Agenda should focus on four steps: building networks of research, facilitating cross-disciplinary collaboration, expanding access to tertiary education, and developing binational and multinational alliances. Starting with the appropriate management tools, universities should develop sound plans and evaluate existing programs and initiatives utilizing dynamic formats. These efforts need to align with institutional priorities, strengths, and strategic goals. Transformational partnerships represent a key vehicle to advance this agenda.[9]

The perspective that the university is a responsible stakeholder has been questioned by those who argue that the rise of the university as a corporate structure creates major roadblocks to building just and inclusive communities. This is not a minor criticism, as cities and their regions face the challenges of a post-COVID-19 pandemic era, a generalized crisis of representation, legacies of racism and colonialism, climate change, health disparities, and long-standing shortages in housing, food supply, and other basic needs.[10]

While universities often report having a positive economic impact on their regions, their role in effectively working to promote more equitable growth in their communities has become a focus of

---
[8] Carnegie Mellon University Sustainability Initiative, "2020 Voluntary University Review."
[9] Cabrera and Cutright, *Higher Education and SDG17*.
[10] Ariel Armony and Ann E. Cudd, *Toward a Post-Pandemic Higher Education System* (Routledge, 2022), 302–15.

concern.¹¹ Critics stress that HEIs have become a powerful actor in urban governance, having emerged as the dominant employer, real estate holder, health-care provider, and even agent of policing.¹² Furthermore, the physical expansion of universities often results in higher housing costs and the displacement of lower-income residents. Critics have also noted that the university's claim to advance a social justice mission – for example, under the framework of the SDGs – is often contradictory to the institution's position vis-à-vis its employees' working conditions and well-being.¹³

The link between universities and the SDG agenda is not only grounded in the capabilities of HEIs, but also in the ethical responsibility of universities serving their local communities and adhering to values that align with the needs of global communities.¹⁴ Linking the utilitarian demands of these institutions and their ethical ideals requires universities to design strategies for engagement that address both the imperatives posed by today's knowledge economy and their commitment to extend prosperity and well-being to society at large.¹⁵ This requirement is particularly relevant for SDG16 – on Peace, Justice, and Strong Institutions – because sustainable and inclusive development is inextricably linked to good governance, robust and resilient rule of law, independent civil society, and the protection of human dignity.

---

¹¹ Anna Valero and John Van Reenen, "The Economic Impact of Universities: Evidence from Across the Globe," *Economics of Education Review* 68 (2019): 53–67; Ted Van Green, "Republicans Increasingly Critical of Several Major U.S. Institutions, Including Big Corporations and Banks," Pew Research Center, August 20, 2021, https://www.pewresearch.org/short-reads/2021/08/20/republicans-increasingly-critical-of-several-major-u-s-institutions-including-big-corporations-and-banks/.

¹² Davarian L. Baldwin, *In the Shadow of the Ivory Tower: How Universities Are Plundering Our Cities* (Bold Type Books, 2021).

¹³ Paul Benneworth, "So What Is a University in Any Case? A Grass-Roots Perspective on the University and Urban Social Justice," in *Hope Under Neoliberal Austerity: Responses from Civil Society and Civic Universities*, eds. Mel Steer, Simin Davoudi, Mark Shucksmith, and Liz Todd (Bristol University Press, 2021), 251–56.

¹⁴ Liz Todd, Simin Davoudi, Mark Shucksmith, and Mel Steer, "The Civic University: Introduction," in *Hope Under Neoliberal Austerity: Responses from Civil Society and Civic Universities* (Policy Press, 2021), 147–52.

¹⁵ Armony and Cudd, *Toward a Post-Pandemic Higher Education System*.

In the United States, public trust in HEIs has been in decline for some time. According to Gallup polling, Americans' confidence in higher education has dropped drastically during the past eight years. In 2023, 22% of respondents expressed "very little" confidence in colleges and universities, up from 9% in 2015, while 36% of respondents had "a great deal" or "quite a lot" of confidence in higher education, down from 57% in 2015.[16] Other surveys have shown similar trends, indicating that public opinion has increasingly questioned whether colleges and universities have a positive effect on their communities, regions, and the country's well-being.[17] There is also a growing chorus of voices – from within and outside of universities – that speak critically "about the objectivity, legitimacy, and accuracy of the academy as a locus of truth and facts."[18]

Both those with and without college degrees question how well-equipped they are to succeed in the 21st century workplace. Part of this sharp decline in confidence and uncertainty around the value of a college degree is likely due to the rising costs of postsecondary education and/or difficulty gaining access to four-year institutions.[19] Some factors that may have eroded public trust in higher education include attacks by conservative politicians, the effects of disrupted learning and traditional university life due to COVID-19, and numerous public controversies and scandals around admissions which has reinforced the idea that higher education is only for the wealthy and elite.[20]

In late 2023 and early 2024, US colleges and universities are also being widely criticized because of their responses to the

---

[16] Megan Brenan, "Americans' Confidence in Higher Education Down Sharply," Gallup, July 17, 2023, https://news.gallup.com/poll/508352/americans-confidence-higher-education-down-sharply.aspx.

[17] Van Green, "Republicans Increasingly Critical."

[18] Ronald J. Daniels, *What Universities Owe Democracy* (Johns Hopkins University Press, 2021).

[19] Brenan, "Americans' Confidence"; Sarah Wood, "Americans Have Less Confidence in Higher Ed: Why?" *U.S. News*, August 7, 2023, https://www.usnews.com/education/best-colleges/applying/articles/americans-have-less-confidence-in-higher-education.

[20] Michael T. Nietzel, "Americans' confidence in higher education sinks to a new low," *Forbes*, July 11, 2023, https://www.forbes.com/sites/michaelnietzel/2023/07/11/americans-confidence-in-higher-education-sinks-to-a-new-low/.

Israel-Hamas war. HEIs have experienced tense disputes on their campuses, from protests to threats on students. *The New York Times*'s Michelle Goldberg has cogently argued that the complexity of the situation "should make it an ideal subject to teach critical thinking and how to have difficult discussions," but the result has been very different, in fact, she contends that "it is being used as a toxin that threatens the entire academic enterprise."[21] Universities in the United States have struggled to foster debate while embracing a diversity of views, impairing their capacity to serve as an inclusive place for discussion of critical social and political issues. In other words, HEIs have shown poor performance in fostering conversations across different perspectives, arguably a fundamental component of their mission as educational institutions.

If universities want to play a meaningful role in elevating the relevance and effectiveness of the SDG agenda to solve public policy problems, they need to align their mission with their place in their local community and the global challenges we face today. The problems Higher Education has fostering meaningful dialogues that engage a variety of perspectives are compounded by the serious challenges facing democracies at large, which are not delivering equitably for large sectors of their populations. Even though this scenario is pessimistic, adopting the SDGs (and linking this agenda to the framework of human rights, as discussed below) provides an opportunity to reinvent the ways we address urgent challenges in communities across the world, while also contributing to building a new future for HEIs.

THE SDGs: GUIDING PRINCIPLE FOR A NEW HUMAN RIGHTS AGENDA?

Scholars have argued that embracing the role of the university as an institution committed to the public good requires a decision to

---

[21] Michelle Goldberg, "When it Comes to Israel, Who Decides What You Can and Can't Say?" *The New York Times*, November 4, 2023, https://www.nytimes.com/2023/11/04/opinion/sunday/israel-palestine-speech-debate.html.

move toward a new paradigm based on social responsibility, ethical engagement, and reciprocity.[22] As universities seek to reimagine themselves and deliver this paradigm shift, they need to identify and develop best practices concerning curriculum changes, institutional commitments, and internal reorganization. They must also engage in frank conversations regarding the future role of US colleges and universities in enabling democratic practices to thrive within an increasingly fragmented and violent society.[23]

A new paradigm should reinvent the field of human rights by combining the SDG and human rights agendas in innovative ways. This is a vital opportunity for universities. As Sarah Mendelson writes, reflecting the views of a burgeoning Community of Practice, "Innovations in higher education offer a pathway to advance the closely aligned endeavors of creating peaceful, just, and inclusive communities. Universities have a critical role to play in generating a refreshed approach to human rights that includes SDG literacy."[24] Building a "human rights action plan" dovetails with the SDG agenda because, as established by the Universal Declaration of Human Rights, civil and political rights alongside economic, social, and cultural rights, are indivisible and interdependent. As Volker Türk has argued, any attempt to separate these rights is detrimental to advancing a genuine human rights agenda.[25] The

---

[22] Sarah E. Mendelson, "Paradigm shift: Creating more just societies with the SDGs, human rights, and innovations in higher education," *The SDG Second Half: Ideas for Doing Things Differently*, April 5, 2023, Brookings Institution, https://www.brookings.edu/articles/paradigm-shift-creating-more-just-societies-with-the-sdgs-human-rights-and-innovations-in-higher-education/; Emiliano Bosio and Gustavo Gregorutti, *The Emergence of the Ethically-Engaged University* (Palgrave Macmillan, 2023).

[23] Mellon Foundation, "Call for Concepts: Exploring Democracy, Environmental Justice, and Social Justice," 2023, https://www.mellon.org/article/call-for-concepts-higher-learning-2024?utm_source=biweekly&utm_medium=email&utm_campaign=november_2_23.

[24] Sarah E. Mendelson, "Synthesis Document – Toward a Paradigm Shift: Creating a Community of Practice on Human Rights and the Sustainable Development Goals," Carnegie Mellon University, June 22, 2023, https://www.heinz.cmu.edu/faculty-research/profiles/mendelson-sarah/postbellagiooutcomedocumentcommunityofpracticesddsgandhumanrights.pdf.

[25] Türk, *Human Rights Are Antidote to Prevailing Politics*.

SDGs can help reinvigorate and renew human rights education by localizing specific rights and translating them to particular contexts. This framework is necessary to bring human rights to local communities, address social justice gaps, as well as retool policies and how progress is measured.[26]

The responsibility of universities to advance the SDGs is part of their "indispensable role in the exercise of building, maintaining, and inspiring liberal democracy." This is particularly germane to the research university, which "weaves together the four connections to democracy – social mobility, civic education, stewardship of facts, and pluralism."[27] These functions are essential to an integrated SDG and human rights agenda.

THE SDGs: A MARKETING TOOL?

Universities operate in a highly competitive environment. They are continuously vying for public recognition while devoting significant efforts to improve their rankings and prestige, particularly in comparison to their peers.[28] University impact rankings that evaluate the extent to which academic institutions have successfully mainstreamed the SDGs into their strategies have gained significant attention in recent years and influenced institutional strategies, reputations, and stakeholders' perceptions.

However, a growing number of studies have explored the relationship between such university rankings and their alignment with the SDGs, focusing specifically on the accuracy of those rankings in capturing universities' sustainable development efforts. They also discuss the implications of these rankings on HEIs and propose methods to improve the quality of these university ranking systems in assessing SDGs.[29] Research to date indicates that university sustainability rankings, while influential, may not adequately capture HEIs'

---

[26] Mendelson, "Paradigm shift."
[27] Daniels, *What Universities Owe Democracy*.
[28] Cabrera and Cutright, *Higher Education and SDG17*.
[29] Walter Leal Filho et al, "A Framework for the Implementation of the Sustainable Development Goals in University Programmes," *Journal of Cleaner Production* 299 (2021).

comprehensive efforts toward sustainable development. Inconsistencies in evaluation criteria, indicators, and methodologies across ranking systems lead to ranking discrepancies and limited alignment with the SDGs.[30] Improvements in transparency, inclusion of qualitative indicators, automation of indicator mapping processes, and collaboration among ranking organizations are recommended to enhance alignment with the SDGs.[31] Further research and diversified research methodologies are necessary to address the complexities and challenges associated with assessing HEIs' performance vis-à-vis the 2030 Agenda and their alignment with sustainable development. The most attention has been paid to outlining better practices for implementing SDGs and standardizing frameworks through which successful SDG implementation can be assessed within university ranking systems to facilitate accurate institutional comparisons.

For example, the Times Higher Education Impact Ranking (THE-IR), a global sustainability ranking for HEIs, has received significant attention from the global academic community.[32] The THE-IR is a comprehensive assessment of HEIs' contributions toward the SDGs based on four different areas: research, stewardship, outreach, and teaching. As of 2023, the highest-ranked countries in the THE-IR were the United Kingdom, Australia, and Canada. While over 90 countries submitted to THE-IR assessments in 2023, researchers have argued that the THE-IR only helps academic leaders evaluate "just how difficult it is to classify and inventory work under each goal, capture the extent of their university's engagement with the goals, and, perhaps most importantly, accelerate commitment and actions."[33]

---

[30] Bautista-Puig et al, "Enhancing Sustainable Development Goals"; Galleli et al, "Sustainability University Rankings."

[31] Anwaar Buzaboon et al, "Automated Mapping of Environmental Higher Education Ranking Systems Indicators to SDGs Indicators using Natural Language Processing and Document Similarity," *2021 International Conference on Innovation and Intelligence for Informatics, Computing, and Technologies (3ICT)* (2021): 170–74.

[32] Times Higher Education, "Impact Rankings 2023," https://www.timeshighereducation.com/impactrankings.

[33] Cabrera and Cutright, *Higher Education and SDG17*; Ross, "Higher Education's Role."

For example, Bautista-Puig, Orduña-Malea, and Perez-Esparrells find that the THE-IR does not effectively capture universities' comprehensive impact on the SDGs. Using summative content analysis of THE-IR web-scraped data from 2019, 2020, and 2021, they conclude that because THE-IR evaluations are based upon universities' highest performing SDG benchmarks, the areas of emphasis in the resulting performance rankings varied significantly across individual SDGs for all institutions, including those institutions with the highest rankings.[34]

Using an explanatory case study approach, Derakhshan, Hassanzadeh, and Nekoofar arrived at similar findings. They identified divergence across sustainability-related ranking systems and concluded that university impact ratings are insufficient in identifying institutions that positively influence their societies by achieving the SDGs.[35] Comparative analyses of different sustainability ranking systems have also concluded that their reliability in evaluating university sustainability efforts is questionable at best. These difficulties in goal classification and progress tracking have led several scholars to advocate for greater transparency and standardization within and across sustainability ranking systems.[36] Specifically, they call for limiting the use of THE-IR in decision making until a more comprehensive and reliable evaluation framework for sustainability efforts is developed, one that includes qualitative and quantitative indicators.

---

[34] Núria Bautista-Puig, Enrique Orduña-Malea, and Carmen Perez-Esparrells, "Enhancing Sustainable Development Goals or Promoting Universities? An Analysis of the Times Higher Education Impact Rankings," *International Journal of Sustainability in Higher Education* 23, no. 8 (2022): 211–31.

[35] Maryam Derakhshan, Mohammad Hassanzadeh, and Mohammad H. Nekoofar, "A Cross Analysis of Impact University Ranking System," *International Journal of Information Science and Management (IJISM)* 19, no. 1 (2021): 87–98.

[36] Barbara Galleli et al, "Sustainability University Rankings: A Comparative Analysis of UI green metric and the Times Higher Education World University Rankings," *International Journal of Sustainability in Higher Education* 23, no. 2 (2022): 404–25.

Improving the reliability of SDG assessment tools like THE-IR is essential because HEIs are in a strong position to bring about the broader cultural shifts required to successfully implement sustainability practices, which fundamentally requires adherence to non-monetary purposes and incentives that cannot happen without these shifts.[37] While the incorporation of SDGs into university ranking systems has resulted in many HEIs emphasizing their sustainability efforts in order to market themselves to a more and more sustainability-conscious clientele, these efforts fall short of incorporating clear, transparent, and accountable sustainability visions; robust shared governance structures; and inclusive community engagement initiatives into all aspects of their operations. Since there are many different types of HEIs, their purposes need to be specific and so should their reporting on sustainability efforts.[38]

CONCLUSION: THREE PILLARS

The interconnection between human rights and the SDGs underscores that inclusive economic development and social justice are inextricably linked to good governance, robust and resilient rule of law, independent civil society, and the protection of human dignity. The interdependency between civil and political rights and economic, social, and cultural rights is as relevant to the 2030 Agenda as it is to the Universal Declaration of Human Rights adopted over 75 years ago.[39] SDG 16, the focus of this volume, which is explored in detail by other contributors, offers an opportunity for universities to leverage the connections and networks they have built over decades to co-create solutions with their communities and address socio-economic imbalances that hinder the goals of building peace, more just societies, and strong institutions.

---

[37] Fabio Caputo, Lorenzo Ligorio, and Simone Pizzi, "The Contribution of Higher Education Institutions to the SDGs – An Evaluation of Sustainability Reporting Practices," *Administrative Sciences* 11, no. 3 (2021).
[38] Luis Alberto Mejía-Manzano et al, "An Exploratory Study Examining the Key Aspects and Actions for Universities to Achieve High Sustainability Rankings," *Sustainability* 15, no. 5 (2023).
[39] Türk, *Human Rights Are Antidote to Prevailing Politics*.

The work ahead is complex. As some universities embark on these paradigm shifts, there are three pillars that deserve particular attention as we think about the role of HEIs in advancing the SDGs, as well as how to train the next generation of public policy experts and engaged scholars through the context of the SDG agenda.[40]

A focus on interactions between SDG targets is a critical component of any concerted effort to advance the 2030 Agenda in a university setting. Universities should first address the problems of siloed structures, single discipline thinking, and compartmentalized operations. In addition to structural and organizational changes, HEIs also need to find innovative ways to inspire and guide educators, administrators, researchers, staff, and students in advancing sustainable development. The promotion of "SDG synergies" offers a roadmap for multiple initiatives, including curriculum development, teaching approaches, institutional policies, and community engagement.[41] This task is an essential and innovative component to help train the next generation of practitioners in this field. It is, however, not necessary to start from scratch. There are plenty of existing models that demonstrate the integration of sustainability practices into the university's operations, communications, and engagement, such as the integration of a climate change and carbon emissions framework into university strategic planning.[42] Other models include interdisciplinary collaborative networks that concentrate on research and teaching in

---

[40] "The world's goals to save humanity are hugely ambitious – but they are still the best option," *Nature* 621 (2023): 227–29.

[41] "The world's goals to save humanity"; Paulo R. M. Correia and Ian M. Kinchin, "Pedagogic Resonance and Threshold Concepts to Access the Hidden Complexity of Education for Sustainability," in *Higher Education for Sustainable Development Goals*, eds. Carolina Machado and João Paulo Davim (River Publisher, 2022), 1–22.

[42] Thomas Owen-Smith, "Integrating Climate into Strategy and Planning in Universities," SUMS Consulting, 2023, https://sums.org.uk/app/uploads/2023/10/Integrating-climate-into-strategy-and-planning-in-universities_vf.pdf.; Brooke Hansen, Peter Stiling, and Whitney Fung Uy, "Innovations and Challenges in SDG Integration and Reporting in Higher Education: A Case Study from the University of South Florida," *International Journal of Sustainability in Higher Education* 22, no. 5 (2021): 1002–21.

and concerning the global south; teams that bring together researchers in environmental archeology, sustainability, business, and other fields; and sustainability-focused learning communities.[43]

This volume emphasizes the notion that "many of the SDGs address and elevate socioeconomic rights, which in turn, when implemented, can engage local communities and community leaders, make human rights more relevant for people, and improve lives."[44] In alignment with this idea, a second pillar of this volume is based on the notion that "local communities, not national governments, are often the front lines for developing rights-based approaches to socioeconomic challenges."[45]

Localities differ greatly in terms of accessible social justice data for community members, government officials, scholars, and practitioners. Data gaps and lags, particularly when it comes to disaggregated data by gender, race, and geographical boundaries, make it extremely difficult to identify who is falling behind in cities. Academic institutions can be vital in bolstering the ability to apply data science to address this critical challenge. We must determine how to better use the data we already have and establish more direct and mutually beneficial relationships with local stakeholders so that they can participate in the data-creation process. New models of community engagement can help close data gaps and develop more effective strategies to share information with policy makers. Universities should pay attention to local populations, pose pertinent questions, and assemble diverse, multidisciplinary teams. Establishing confidence between HEIs and local communities is essential.[46]

Advancing justice in the context of SDG 16 often requires working on problems as defined by the community in order to localize the actual challenges they face.[47] Universities have the capacity

---

[43] Godwell Nhamo and Vuyo Mjimba, *Sustainable Development Goals and Institutions of Higher Education* (Springer Cham, 2020).
[44] Mendelson, "Synthesis Document."
[45] Mendelson, "Synthesis Document."
[46] Mendelson, "Synthesis Document."
[47] As an example of a specific challenge faced by a community, see: Center for Analytical Approaches to Social Innovation, "Allegheny County Policing Project (ACPP)," University of Pittsburgh, 2021, https://www.caasi.pitt.edu/initiatives/allegheny-county-policing-project-acpp.

to embrace a "place-based" role and help facilitate social justice. As a result, universities can maximize the benefits of economic investments and opportunities for their communities to ensure that under-resourced, vulnerable, and underserved populations do not continue to be left behind.[48]

The third task for universities is to assess progress regarding the 2030 Agenda. This requires that they identify a suitable framework to assist them in the implementation of the SDGs. Institutionally, universities need to establish policies, strategies, plans, and governing structures to support mainstreaming the SDGs into their operations. Thematically, HEIs should support interdisciplinarity and the exploration of a variety of topics, widening the scope of subjects to address a greater number of SDGs, as well as diversifying themes to cover multiple SDGs at once. Structurally, HEIs should provide the necessary resources, equipment, materials, and operational support toward SDG implementation. Lastly, at the individual level, universities must facilitate and encourage concern, awareness, and commitment to the SDG agenda and equip their faculty, staff, and students with the necessary tools to advance a coordinated and effective sustainability agenda.[49] As noted, a key dimension of this task is to work with local communities to create "people-centered data ecosystems, including open-source data portals" aimed at creating solutions to enhance rights for all.[50]

These three pillars – SDG synergies, trust and collaboration between HEIs and local communities, and progress tracking and assessment informed by data generated with community input – provide a roadmap for how to use the SDGs to teach, train,

---

[48] John Goddard and Paul Vallance, *The University and the City* (Routledge, 2013); UPP Foundation, "Truly Civic: Strengthening the Connection between Universities and Their Places," UPP Foundation, 2019, https://upp-foundation.org/wp-content/uploads/2019/02/Civic-University-Commission-Final-Report.pdf.

[49] Leal Filho et al, "A framework for the implementation."

[50] Elizabeth Andersen and Sarah Mendelson, "Room 16: #JustRecovery – Toward the Universal Advancement of Accountable, Inclusive, People-Centered Social and Justice Policies in the Post-COVID-19 era," Brookings Institution, 2021, https://www.brookings.edu/wp-content/uploads/2021/11/2021-Room-documents_Room16.pdf; Mendelson, "Synthesis Document."

partner, and advance new agendas that position universities as responsible, place-based stakeholders, and connect people, information, and policies in more effective ways. The interconnection of the human rights framework and the 2030 Agenda places social justice at the center of the health of democracy and creates an unprecedented opportunity for HEIs to re-energize efforts aimed at socio-economic renewal in cities and regions in the United States and around the world.

ACKNOWLEDGMENTS

This chapter was written with the collaboration of Stephanie Confer, Michaela Cushing-Daniels, and Krystal Marsh. I would like to thank them for their extraordinary work.

6

BETWEEN LOCALIZATION AND REALIZATION: PARTNERSHIPS TOWARD ADVANCING HUMAN RIGHTS AND THE SUSTAINABLE DEVELOPMENT GOALS IN LOS ANGELES

Gaea Morales[a], Anthony Tirado Chase[b], Michelle E. Anderson[a] and Sofia Gruskin[a]

[a]*University of Southern California, USA*
[b]*Occidental College, USA*

ABSTRACT

What does the relationship between the Sustainable Development Goals (SDGs) and human rights look like in practice at the local level? With Los Angeles as a case study, we focus on the partnership between universities and the Mayor's Office in the localization of the 2030 Agenda for Sustainable Development. The co-creation of student "Task Forces" with city officials and the evolution of the use of the Goals in planning over time demonstrate how localization created opportunities to identify and act on human rights issues through SDG implementation at the city level.

Keywords: Human rights; Sustainable Development Goals; city-academic partnerships; localization; task forces; data

INTRODUCTION: THE SDGs AND HUMAN RIGHTS AT THE LOCAL LEVEL

In a 2018 keynote address, then-Los Angeles Mayor Eric Garcetti launched the Los Angeles Sustainable Development Goals (L.A. SDGs), a city-wide effort to translate and implement the United Nations SDGs and the broader 2030 Agenda in L.A. City.[1] Los Angeles was one of the first cities in the world to commit to the localization of the SDG framework. By 2024, according to U.N.-Habitat, over 196 local and regional governments have produced Voluntary Local Reviews (VLRs), reports documenting local-level progress on the goals and showcasing local initiatives to implement the global goals.[2] While illustrating the importance of taking on these global challenges locally, Garcetti quoted Eleanor Roosevelt speaking to the UN Commission on Human Rights: "'Where, after all, do basic universal human rights begin? In small places...' Without concerned citizen action to uphold these human rights close to home, we shall look in vain for progress in the larger world."[3] Nearly five years since Los Angeles' launch, and with just over six years remaining until 2030, we return to these words and closely explore the links between human rights and the SDGs in the context of partnerships between city government and academic institutions in the local implementation of the 2030 Agenda.

---

[1] Occidental College, "Mayor Garcetti Announces Partnership with Occidental to Advance Sustainable Development Goals," February 5, 2018, https://www.oxy.edu/academics/global-engagement/young-initiative/speakers-events/mayor-garcetti-announces-partnership.

[2] UN-Habitat, "Our Approach | Localizing the SDGs," https://sdglocalization.org/our-approach.

[3] *Global Ambition, Local Action - Keynote Address by Mayor Eric Garcetti at Occidental College*, 2018, https://www.youtube.com/watch?v=Je_wx-PUgtI.

The SDGs provide a common platform to measure progress toward peace and prosperity at global, national, and local levels on pressing issues. The 17 interrelated goals are meant to be achieved by 2030, but according to UN officials, this aspiration is "in peril."[4] In theory, this set of goals aims to promote sustainable development across social, economic, and environmental spheres. Unlike its predecessor, the Millennium Development Goals (MDGs), the SDGs explicitly recognize that inequalities exist within, and not just across, countries. Furthermore, they exemplify how sustainable development requires cross-cutting rather than competing goals, with specific targets and measurable indicators. Another major difference between the MDGs and the SDGs lies in the negotiation processes.[5] Stakeholder engagement was central in the drafting stage of the agreement, evidenced by the critical role of Major Groups and other Stakeholders (MGoS) in the development and adoption of the 2030 Agenda. MGoS consisted of nine main sectors, including women and Indigenous peoples, local authorities, and nongovernmental organizations.[6]

The SDGs are notable for expanding the concept of economic development to include attention to inequalities and non-discrimination, as well as a fundamental commitment to monitoring, evaluation, and stakeholder engagement. These contributions demonstrate how the SDG framework itself intersects with existing human rights norms. SDG 16 is one of the few explicit examples of human rights integration in the 2030 agenda, as it aims to "promote peaceful and inclusive societies for sustainable development,

---

[4] Rebecca Geldard and Stefan Ellerbeck, "Are the UN's Sustainable Development Goals on Track?" *World Economic Forum* (blog), September 11, 2023, https://www.weforum.org/agenda/2023/09/un-sustainable-development-goals-progress-report/.

[5] David J. Gordon and Kristin Ljungkvist, "Theorizing the Globally Engaged City in World Politics," *European Journal of International Relations* 28, no. 1 (March 1, 2022): 58–82, https://doi.org/10.1177/13540661211064449.

[6] MGoS-CM, "Major Groups and Other Stakeholders Coordination Mechanism (MGOS-CM) Terms of Reference," December 18, 2020, https://sustainabledevelopment.un.org/content/documents/27114MGoS_TOR18_Dec_2020.pdf.

provide access to justice for all and build effective, accountable and inclusive institutions at all levels," and includes targets on promoting and enforcing "non-discriminatory laws and policies for sustainable development" (16.b) and "develop(ing) effective, accountable, and transparent institutions at all levels" (16.6).[7] More holistically, goals such as those on food (SDG 2), health (SDG 3), education (SDG 4), decent work (SDG 8), and housing (SDG 11) echo human rights embedded in the International Covenant on Economic, Social and Cultural Rights (ICESCR) and other relevant instruments.[8]

Scholars and practitioners alike, however, have critiqued the implicit nature of human rights principles within the context of the SDGs and their implementation. As Bexell et al. write,

> *the SDGs lack systematic references to the core human rights treaties with their related instruments. While the SDGs and human rights address similar issues, such as education, health, welfare, and many others, they build on divergent logics and are constructed differently.*[9]

One of the persistent gaps in SDG implementation, vis-à-vis human rights principles, is a more robust conception of accountability. For example, can and how will duty-bearers be held to account for the implementation (or non-implementation) of their relevant SDG commitments?

While a comprehensive response to this question is beyond the scope of this chapter, we provide key insights into the practice of

---

[7] UN Department of Economic and Social Affairs, "Goal 16 | Department of Economic and Social Affairs," https://sdgs.un.org/goals/goal16#targets_and_indicators.

[8] UN High-Level Political Forum on Sustainable Development, "Summary Table: Linkages between the SDGs and Human Rights," https://hlpf.un.org/tools/summary-table-linkages-between-the-sdgs-and-human-rights.

[9] Magdalena Bexell, Thomas Hickmann, and Andrea Schapper, "Strengthening the Sustainable Development Goals through Integration with Human Rights," *International Environmental Agreements: Politics, Law and Economics* 23, no. 2 (June 1, 2023): 133–39, https://doi.org/10.1007/s10784-023-09605-x.

linking human rights and the SDGs at the local level. Localization, a growing trend in work on the SDGs, gives us a useful point of entry to contribute to this debate. As with virtually all UN frameworks, the SDGs were conceived to apply at the national level. They were adopted by UN member states and call for implementation at national levels; monitoring of their indicators is largely based on data produced by national statistical systems. And yet, increasingly, entities that are not national governments are voluntarily engaging in the SDG framework, including numerous cities (as well as universities and the private sector). We propose that focusing on the city level, including both city government and community actors, gives a unique vantage point in understanding the relationship and potential of linking the SDGs and human rights. This chapter, thus, shifts the focus from the national to the city level. We pay particular attention to the case of Los Angeles, where there has been considerable engagement by city actors with the SDGs. How has that intersected with human rights in policy and practice, and what broader lessons can be taken from such intersections?

Global human rights standards and norms have developed over decades to provide both a legal anchor and social imaginary that directs how governments interact with individuals and populations. We argue that, despite fair critiques of the SDG framework's refusal to explicitly engage human rights at their onset, the process of SDG localization simultaneously makes clear the need to identify and act on human rights at the city level if SDG-based goals are to be met. Indeed, both the Danish Institute for Human Rights and the UN's Office of the High Commissioner for Human Rights have mapped ways that the SDGs and human rights can and should reinforce each other.[10] Specifically, in the case of Los Angeles, SDG localization has provided city actors with a baseline understanding

---

[10] "The UDHR at 75: A Conversation with UN High Commissioner for Human Rights Volker Türk," CSIS Human Rights Initiative, April 18, 2023, https://www.csis.org/events/udhr-75-conversation-un-high-commissioner-human-rights-volker-turk. See also "The Human Rights Guide to the Sustainable Development Goals," The Danish Institute for Human Rights Methodology, https://sdg.humanrights.dk/sites/sdg.humanrights.dk/files/SDG%20database%20methodology_0.pdf.

of how and where public services need to be strengthened, with particular attention to underserved communities. This focus has shown the need for more explicit attention to human rights standards and how they may be embedded in policies and various institutions in order to address gaps that have been identified so that the SDGs can be achieved. Thus, while both the SDGs and human rights are traditionally seen as independent international frameworks, they may be better understood as frameworks that are more likely achieved when conceptualized as interdependent. Localization of the SDGs in Los Angeles – accompanied (as we shall explain) by the growth of city-academic partnerships – precisely demonstrates this potential.

LOS ANGELES AND THE SDGs

Whose Efforts?

What has L.A. City done to move toward the SDGs and its targets as well as achieve human rights standards? To answer this question, it is important to first define who we talk about when we talk about "the city." Scholars across disciplines have defined the city in different ways, from a hub, to actors not unlike the nation-state.[11] For our purposes, when we talk about the city's actions or efforts, we are talking about the city as government: consisting of multiple offices and departments, and the individuals that comprise them. We make this separation so that we can distinguish between SDG or human rights localization as a process by government actors, and localization by other actors that inhabit the city, which range from grassroots activists to private actors from the academic and industrial sectors. Furthermore, by defining the city as an organization, we can speak more precisely about the relationship between formal institutions and individuals, and dynamic processes of leadership, decision-making, and agenda-setting.

---

[11] Gordon and Ljungkvist, "Theorizing the Globally Engaged City"; Saskia Sassen, "On Concentration and Centrality in the Global City," in *World Cities in a World-System*, eds. Paul L. Knox and Peter J. Taylor (Cambridge University Press, 1995), 63–76, https://doi.org/10.1017/CBO9780511522192.005.

For the remainder of this section, we describe the case of Los Angeles in the broader context of the SDGs and embedded human rights norms. We begin with a brief overview of the SDGs in L.A., with a focus on the component of city-academic partnerships and "Task Forces" (TFs). We then focus on two key dimensions of the localization process: (1) TFs as a means to promote human rights; and (2) TFs as a means to strengthen capacity to address further challenges. In doing so, we highlight how the SDGs and human rights protection as well as advancement are linked in Los Angeles, citing both challenges and best practices.

City-Academic Partnerships: Introducing the Task Forces

Launched in 2018, the SDGs in L.A. is a multi-phase, multilateral project aimed at adopting and adapting the Goals across Los Angeles. It originated as a collaborative effort between the Mayor's Office, Mayor Eric Garcetti, and the Conrad N. Hilton Foundation. Efforts to achieve progress on the 2030 Agenda have since been explicit and well-publicized by the L.A. City government, spearheaded by staff of the Mayor's Office of International Affairs (MOIA). The VLRs are a key symbol of these efforts, as well as tools to engage with other cities, within and beyond the United States, with similar objectives. In 2019, L.A. was the first city to present a VLR that did not simply match SDG targets and indicators to existing city-level performance standards. L.A.'s VLR process included a nearly year-long, in-depth mapping strategy that categorized standards that were directly applicable, needed only slight modifications (e.g., to disaggregate from national to local level data), or were not applicable to the city context. The translated standards were then compared against existing L.A. city data to measure and present progress on indicators.[12]

The VLR itself, and the SDG efforts in L.A., were not isolated to city actors. Though one of the major outcomes, the VLR is only one product of ongoing partnerships between city and academic actors. These partnerships have taken the form of what we

---

[12] City of L.A. Sustainable Development Goals, "Voluntary Local Review," https://sdg.lacity.gov/our-work/voluntary-local-review.

call "TFs." While TFs are in themselves not innovative, as they have long proliferated across private and public sectors, we have a particular concept of TFs in the context of the SDGs in L.A. TFs are student research groups conducting fixed-term, problem-driven, and policy-oriented research, guided by academic advisors and overseen by a client, in this case, local government.[13]

Through the leadership of the MOIA and in partnership with various city departments, over 160 undergraduate and graduate students have participated in over 22 research projects in support of implementing and advancing various SDG targets. Broadly, the project teams play a key role in assisting the City to identify gaps in aligning plans and practices while highlighting cross-cutting issue areas for mobilizing multi-stakeholder partnerships. Since 2018, the City has partnered with multiple universities, including the John Parke Young Initiative at Occidental College, Arizona State University's Thunderbird School of Global Management, the Luskin School of Public Affairs at University of California Los Angeles, Pomona College, and the Institute on Inequalities in Global Health at the University of Southern California.

TFs have generally fallen within six key models or purposes: exploratory or mapping, stakeholder engagement, data assessment and collection, landscape analysis, best practice case studies, and proposals and recommendations (Fig. 6.1). Beyond structure, TFs have covered a vast array of themes and issue areas, grounded in the SDG framework, ranging from addressing poverty and homelessness to tackling climate change and advancing racial equity and justice.

---

[13] Madeleine Baer and Heidi Nichols Haddad, "Localizing the International Relations Classroom: Evaluation of Academic Partnerships with City Government," *International Studies Perspectives* 24, no. 3 (August 1, 2023): 231–47, https://doi.org/10.1093/isp/ekac008; Gaea Morales, Erin Bromaghim, Angela Kim, Caroline Diamond, Alejo Magginni, Avery Everhart, Sofia Gruskin, and Anthony Tirado Chase, "Classroom Walls and City Hall: Mobilizing Local Partnerships to Advance the Sustainable Development Agenda," *Sustainability* 13, no. 11 (January 2021): 6173, https://doi.org/10.3390/su13116173.

L.A. Task Force Models

Exploratory or Mapping
Broad comparison of city policies, plan, data availability vs. international agreements and datasets.

Stakeholder Engagement
Outreach to gauge interest/issues (public, private, non-profit); expert outreach (academics, policymakers).

Data Assessment & Collection
Review of data made available through client to identify gaps in services and data transparency itself.

Landscape Analysis
Detailed but broad assessment of issue-specific policies, services, access.

Best Practice Case Studies
Rich case study research on successful practices that can be transferred or translated to local context.

Proposals & Recommendations
Direct request for recommendations or contributions on a specific issue/project/question.

Fig. 6.1. Summary of Task Force Models as Presented by Morales, Chase, and Gruskin at the Carnegie Mellon Workshop on the Margins of the World Justice Forum 2022.

The TFs and Human Rights Promotion

There have been TFs that have dealt explicitly with human rights translation and implementation within the SDGs framework, and one such example is "the Wicked Problems" practicum, spearheaded by the Institute on Inequalities in Global Health at the University of Southern California in the Fall semester of 2018. The practicum, the name of which draws from the original term from design theorists Rittel and Webber, sought to address the challenge of not only integrating or mapping existing human rights conventions and treaties onto the SDG framework, but also revising understandings of SDG implementation and measurement to include explicit attention to human rights targets.[14] Given the breadth of the SDG framework, the practicum focused on the issue of homelessness, and whether and how the SDGs are equipped to target this challenge. In addition to the reports documenting links between the SDGs and human rights principles, one key contribution of the TF was to highlight a human rights-based approach to advancing the

---

[14] Horst W. J. Rittel and Melvin M. Webber, "Dilemmas in a General Theory of Planning," *Policy Sciences* 4, no. 2 (1973): 155–69.

SDGs by framing city actors, and not just national-level officials, as duty-bearers.

There have been other TFs that, though not as explicitly tasked with addressing human rights, have also paved the way for further equity- and human rights-driven initiatives. For example, the earliest TF with Occidental College was tasked broadly with understanding how to map or align the goals with existing city-level policies in Los Angeles. Participating students brought up the potential to expand SDG 5 on gender equality, due to its binary conception of gender (i.e., women and men, girls and boys). Within the year, Los Angeles had responded with initiatives that advanced gender-inclusive language, such as in city government job postings and other employment documentation. Six years from the first TF, L.A. is one of the founders of "CHANGE–City Hub and Network for Gender Equity" (CHANGE Network) which "believes that to be successful, [city governments'] work must explicitly recognize and address intersecting inequalities predicated upon race, religion, ethnic origin, disability, sexual orientation, and gender identity or expression."[15] These innovations were accompanied by another set of joint TFs led by Occidental College and Pomona College, which involved working with the CHANGE Network to advance menstrual equity, grounded in conversations emerging from early TFs regarding the limited conceptualization and operationalization of gender equity and justice in SDG 5. At the local government level, Mayor Garcetti signed Executive Directive 35 in August 2022, which extends principles of gender equity beyond city government to contracting and procurement strategies.[16] These examples demonstrate the ripple effect of SDG implementation on initiatives that can serve the promotion and protection of human rights.

City government officials and university partners continue to draw heavily from the findings of the initial mapping of SDGs, and attention to the alignment of existing city policies further highlighted opportunities to expand outcomes along racial and gendered

---

[15] CHANGE, "About," City Hub and Network for Gender Equity, https://www.citieschange.org/about/.

[16] "Executive Directive No. 35 of August 25, 2022, Equitable Access to Contracting Opportunities," Mayor Eric Garcetti, City of Los Angeles.

lines that are not currently accounted for in the SDG framework.[17] Returning again to the work of the Wicked Problems practicum, students and city actors were able to highlight severe disparities bridging SDG 3 on health and well-being and SDG 5 on gender equality by investigating maternal health indicators across race groups. Los Angeles County, and not the City of Los Angeles, holds the primary mandate on public health matters, which presents jurisdictional challenges in acting on health initiatives. However, these lessons addressed the need for more work centering race, in conjunction with gender, as a component of sustainable development. As one of the earliest TFs, the Wicked Problems practicum helped bring human rights principles more directly into the sustainable development agenda and established key questions that continue to drive even the most recent TFs that are explicitly engaging with what it means to realize gender and racial equity within and beyond city government.

The political moment in 2020 amidst George Floyd protests and a collective call to combat systemic racism across and within levels of government institutions further embedded these ideas in the work of SDG implementation. Since 2020, there have been more TFs addressing racial equity and what it means to advance diversity, equity, and justice more broadly at the city level. The lessons from prior TFs, combined with the historic moment of the 2020 summer protests, catalyzed partnerships beyond the MOIA to integrate also the work of the Mayor's Office of Economic Opportunity and the Civil + Human Rights and Equity Department established in 2021.[18]

---

[17] For insights from city partners, see Brenda Shockley, "Racial Justice in Los Angeles: What Can Global Truth-Telling Norms Offer?" and Angela Kim and Erin Bromaghim, "Global Human Rights Norms and City Policy in Los Angeles," both in *Human Rights at the Intersections: Transformation Through Local, Global, and Cosmopolitan Challenges*, eds. Anthony Tirado Chase, Pardis Mahdavi, Hussein Banai, and Sofia Gruskin (1st ed., Bloomsbury Publishing, 2023).

[18] The New York Times, "How George Floyd Died, and What Happened Next." *The New York Times*, July 29, 2022, sec. U.S. https://www.nytimes.com/article/george-floyd.html; The protests of summer of 2020 were a reaction to the murder of George Floyd at the hands of Minneapolis Police Department officers and a broader critique to pervasive institutional rac-

One concrete example is the creation of the Truth-in-Los Angeles project, which was explicitly grounded in SDG 10 on reduced inequalities, SDG 11 on sustainable cities and communities, and SDG 16 on peace, justice, and strong institutions. This TF through Occidental College emerged directly from conversations that began in the summer of 2020 and the growing acceptance within city government of a need for more intentional, city-driven efforts to confront L.A.'s history of racial injustice. The project produced a series of recommendations on how to initiate a truth and accountability process that is responsive to the unique and nuanced history of the city, and that a restorative justice practice requires not just inclusion of, but leadership from, grassroots and civil society actors.

The evolution of TFs through the various partnerships, from their initiation to various "deliverables" (such as reports and recommendations), demonstrates the potential of local SDG implementation to advance the promotion and protection of human rights despite only implicit reference to human rights norms and standards. What these examples make clear is that the city's willingness to consistently and meaningfully engage with community stakeholders, such as universities, colleges, and their students, enabled the greater inclusion of human rights issues and approaches over time.

Measuring Matters: Data and Building Capacity for Human Rights

The City itself, and especially the L.A. SDGs process, has always been driven by data and measuring outcomes. This is most evident in the time and resources allocated to the development of the VLRs and maintenance of the SDGs' reporting platform beginning in 2018.[19] L.A. City invested heavily in building an open-access

---

ism across state and federal agencies in the country.

[19] City of L.A, "City of Los Angeles Indicators for the Sustainable Development Goals," https://sdgdata.lamayor.org/.

reporting platform for SDG indicator data by collating publicly available city- and county-level data across various sources. From the City standpoint, beginning by asking data-driven questions and aligning publicly available disaggregated data with SDG indicators was important for the process of establishing a baseline to measure progress, as well as for securing funding and resources from federal and other agencies that are similarly keen to improve the efficiency and effectiveness of public service delivery. However, the development of the data infrastructure was also key to advancing a human rights agenda more broadly. An understanding not only of baseline progress, but also of patterns in service provision and performance, helps both city officials and the broader community of stakeholders in the city to identify who is left behind, and by how much.

One key example of this process is the Wicked Problems practicum's exploration of Black maternal health in Los Angeles. SDG 3 on good health and well-being proposes a global target for reducing the maternal mortality ratio (3.1.1) to 70 live births per 100,000 by 2030.[20] The L.A. platform uses data at the County level for this particular indicator, due to limited data availability of city-level health indicators given the county's mandate on health (Fig. 6.2).[21] The results, however, remain useful given that L.A. City is the largest of 88 incorporated cities by population, and houses key county health institutions including the Los Angeles General Medical Center (formerly LAC+USC).[22]

According to the data, the maternal mortality ratio (deaths per 100,000 live births) in Los Angeles County has consistently been between 16 and 18 since 2003. However, when comparing L.A. County level data to data disaggregated by race, the results are

---

[20] World Health Organization, "SDG Target 3.1: Reduce the Global Maternal Mortality Ratio to Less than 70 per 100,000 Live Births," https://www.who.int/data/gho/data/themes/topics/topic-details/GHO/sdgtarget3-1-reduce-maternal-mortality.

[21] City of L.A, "Indicator 3.1.1: Maternal mortality ratio," https://sdgdata.lamayor.org/3-1-1/.

[22] County of Los Angeles, "Maps and Geography," https://lacounty.gov/government/about-la-county/maps-and-geography/.

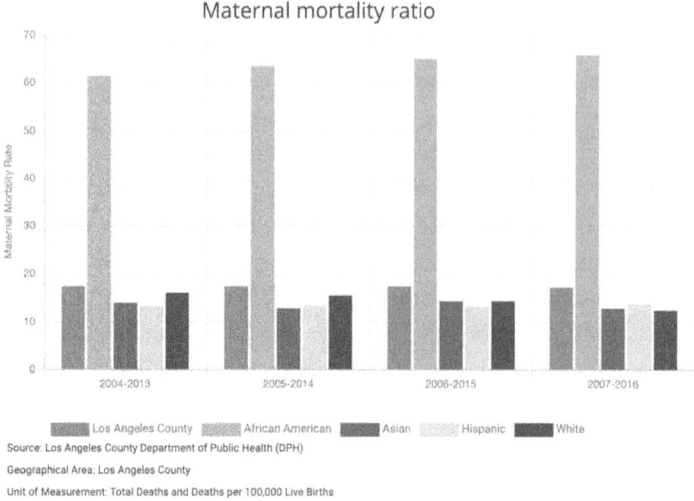

Fig. 6.2. Maternal Mortality Ratio Data from L.A. SDGs Data Reporting Platform.

quite stark. African American women have seen nearly three times the maternal mortality ratio of the county-level aggregate, and of all other racial groups independently from 2004 to 2016.

This example demonstrates the power of data to highlight existing inequalities not just in SDG implementation, but in indicators that are relevant to human rights promotion and protection. However, this data-driven approach is more in line with an inequalities framework, rather than a more holistic engagement of the human rights framework. An inequalities framework prioritizes the discovery of disproportionate burdens and access. This approach is intimately tied to a human rights framework since human rights rely on an understanding of inequality to redress inequalities and injustice in its many forms. In the case of Los Angeles, the City needed to collect data in the early stages of SDG implementation to inform and direct more project-oriented and issue-area focused TFs that supported the various strands of the SDG framework. However, an approach explicitly organized around human rights principles moves beyond inequalities, and requires, at a minimum, six principles: universality, indivisibility, equality and nondiscrimination, participation, and accountability.[23] Thus, discovering and naming inequalities is only one element of bringing human rights to bear in the context of SDG localization. That said, attention to disparities can serve as a springboard for further initiatives that allow for deeper integration of human rights efforts into SDG implementation.

This trajectory is evident in the City's efforts to advance gender equity. In 2021, the City partnered with another TF at Occidental College to develop a set of gender-based indicators for the CHANGE Network. The resulting set of 52 proposed indicators are founded on an explicit recognition of "intersecting inequalities predicated upon race, class, religion, ethnic origin, and disability" and also encourage network members to look "beyond the gender binary."[24] A year later, L.A. City, as one of the co-founders of the CHANGE Network, co-developed a first-of-its-kind Voluntary Gender Review in 2022. The review, which brings together qualitative insights from across the network's members (Barcelona, Buenos Aires, Bogotá, Freetown, London, Los Angeles, and Mexico City), recognized the importance of addressing women's "intersecting marginalized identities such as race or ethnic origin" when assessing vulnerability and the policies put in place to address issues in healthcare and beyond.[25]

---

[23] U.N. Sustainable Development Group, "Human Rights-Based Approach," United Nations Sustainable Development Group, https://unsdg.un.org/2030-agenda/universal-values/human-rights-based-approach.

[24] John Parke Young Initiative on the Global Political Economy, "Measuring Gender Equity in Cities: An Intersectional Set of Proposed Indicators," June 30, 2021, https://www.oxy.edu/academics/global-engagement/young-initiative/research-partnerships-task-forces/measuring-gender-equity.

[25] CHANGE, "CHANGE Voluntary Gender Review," July 1, 2022, https://citieschangeorg.files.wordpress.com/2022/07/change_vgrreport_2022_compressed-2.pdf.

CONCLUSION: REDEFINING STAKEHOLDER ENGAGEMENT FOR THE SDGs AND HUMAN RIGHTS

Human rights have not emerged passively or indirectly from the localization of the sustainable development agenda. This observation is the case even for SDG 10 on inequalities and SDG 16 on peace, justice, and strong institutions, the SDGs most commonly associated with human rights. Findings from various TFs have demonstrated that the SDGs on their own are insufficient in not only measuring, but also advancing human rights norms, especially at the local level. Human rights promotion through SDG localization requires deliberate efforts by actors across both city government and the broader city community. Specifically, future partnerships can benefit from the insight of human rights experts and practitioners, as well as grassroots and civil society actors.

However, we also recognize that human rights framing may look different within the context of the broader city space, namely outside of city government. For example, some city actors may be most concerned with issues around inequalities, while grassroots actors may be more concerned with seeking accountability. City actors may also define human rights priorities differently than other members of the community. These differences may not only result in different perceptions of levels of progress, but also of where the gaps exist, and therefore, where resources should be allocated. These may be direct consequences of larger systems in which governments and other stakeholders operate. City governments often possess their own pre-existing monitoring and evaluation systems that in some ways are more explicitly aligned with an inequalities framework due to their emphasis on measuring performance and gaps. Meanwhile, academics and grassroots or civil society actors may be more in tune with the language of human rights, due to their broader networks and backgrounds. Despite these differences in language, it is important to highlight that various audiences may be working together toward the same goal.

Thus, to achieve human rights and the broader 2030 agenda, the City government–the primary focus of this chapter–must intentionally act in concert with their local communities in all phases of policy development. While activists may be engaging with human rights frameworks in city spaces, such as in the pursuit of environmental justice or bodily autonomy, more can be done to bridge the gap in the ways city governments conceive of sustainable development and human rights principles.

We also recognize that stakeholder engagement must involve more than bilateral partnerships between cities and academia, such as in the TF model. Local community buy-in is key to moving forward from both sustainable development and human rights perspectives. Future TFs can more systematically work to identify processes and mechanisms for meaningful community engagement, and themselves better integrate diverse local perspectives, from the planning stage to its deliverables. Constructive engagements with international frameworks – the SDGs, human rights, and how we propose they can and should intersect – is thus a challenge that requires engaging all relevant stakeholders at all stages and is critical for truly advancing sustainable development.

ACKNOWLEDGMENT

We would also like to acknowledge significant contributions to the chapter from Kelly Wong.

7

UNJUST RECOVERY IN THE WAKE OF THE PANDEMIC AND THE NEED TO REFRAME HUMAN RIGHTS USING THE SDGs

Sarah E. Mendelson

Carnegie Mellon University, USA

ABSTRACT

The hoped-for "just recovery" from the COVID-19 pandemic has not occurred. This chapter examines socioeconomic disparities laid bare by the pandemic in the United States. They have left a marked impression, suggesting that the concept of "American exceptionalism" has negative as well as positive connotations especially when compared with other high-income countries. Strikingly, democracy is not delivering for many Americans, and yet that is not a new situation, as much scholarship shows. These findings challenge received wisdom about how this country is in the aggregate labeled "developed" when many Americans live in conditions similar to or worse than those the World Bank categorizes as "developing." Against this background, the chapter assesses experiential learning models for engaging students on the SDGs

to assess these disparities. While researching social justice gaps in Pittsburgh and Atlanta with Carnegie Mellon students, however, the lack of disaggregated data emerged as a human rights issue and major barrier to fulfilling the SDG principle to "leave no one behind" (LNOB). These findings suggest a paradigm shift is needed, using the SDGs to advance human rights, elevating socioeconomic rights, localizing issues, generating disaggregated data to drive policy recommendations, and scaling up the community of practice that is engaged in this paradigm shift. Field building these aspects of sustainable development has the possibility to positively shape policies, outcomes, and help this democracy actually deliver for all, not just for some. For the United States to lead and bolster human rights and democracy around the world, inequalities at home must be addressed.

Keywords: Sustainable Development Goals; human rights; socioeconomic rights; COVID-19 pandemic; disaggregated data; paradigm shift; experiential learning; leave no one behind

AMERICAN EXCEPTIONALISM IN CONTEXT

The Sustainable Development Goals (SDGs), like the Universal Declaration of Human Rights (UDHR), apply to everyone everywhere. In recent years, since the adoption of the SDGs in 2015, the fact that the SDGs recognize development as a universal phenomenon has led some American global development and foreign policy experts to expand their professional focus from exclusively looking abroad to include the examination of political, economic, and social circumstances in the United States. This shift has also been driven by multiple crises and responses to crises: the pandemic that laid bare the public health disparities in the United States, coupled with the rise of social justice movements after the murder of George Floyd in 2020, plus the election violence of January 6, 2021. The "… distinctions between domestic and foreign policy," Secretary State Antony Blinken noted in his first foreign policy speech, just weeks after January 6, "have simply fallen away. Our domestic renewal and our strength in the world are completely entwined."[1]

The pandemic revealed that classifying and describing the United States as "a developed country" overlooked communities here living in similar or worse conditions as communities in countries the World Bank labels as "developing."[2] As the former Chicago mayor Lori E. Lightfoot noted

> *there are events in history that forcibly reveal the fault lines of a society and the failures of a nation to itself. The COVID-19 crisis in America was such an event, forcing us to confront the abject health care inequality across our cities and communities, as well as the imperative of engaging our democracy to take action.*[3]

Or as the authors of a book on the American response to the pandemic argue "the pandemic told us important, painful truths about who America helps and who it leaves behind, even as it left some people further behind than ever before."[4] Compared to other high-income countries with robust social safety nets, we now know that many Americans are simply not well. Thus, individuals and organizations that have been prompted to join what I think of as a recent and growing "closer-to-home" school are driven by the array of facts concerning the absence of wellbeing for many Americans. The gaps are profoundly at odds with long-held assumptions and beliefs about the functioning of the American system previously taken for

---

[1] Antony J. Blinken, "A Foreign Policy for the American People," State Department, March 3, 2021, available at A Foreign Policy for the American People - United States Department of State.
[2] Daniel Gerszon Mahler, Alaka Holla, and Umar Serajuddin, "Time to Stop Referring to the 'Developing World,'" *World Bank Blogs*, January 23, 2024, https://blogs.worldbank.org/en/opendata/time-stop-referring-developing-world.
[3] Lori E. Lightfoot, "Forward," as cited in David A. Ansell, MD, *The Death Gap: How Inequality Kills* (University of Chicago, 2017, 2021), ix.
[4] Joe Nocera and Bethany McLean, *The Big Fail: What the Pandemic Revealed About Who America Protects and Who It Leaves Behind* (Portfolio/Penguin, 2023), xiii.

granted by researchers and practitioners working on democracy and human rights around the world.[5]

Yet when the pandemic struck and Congress passed the American Rescue Plan Act (ARPA) worth $1.9 trillion enabling $350 billion to flow to states, among other funds, it seemed remotely possible that these funds might drive a just recovery – closing social justice gaps.[6] In summer 2020, as part of the Brookings Institution and The Rockefeller Foundation's flagship "17 Rooms" exercise, as trillions of dollars were being spent around the world, I co-moderated a series of discussions for Room 16 with rights experts, and the questions top of mind were: Will Covid relief and recovery packages lead to a new, just recovery after the pandemic? Will we find a more just or unjust recovery?[7] Specifically, will we find inequalities and social justice gaps that existed pre-Covid, prior to 2020, reduced or eliminated or will they persist? To make the work manageable, the research that emerged from those discussions focused on case studies in Pittsburgh, Atlanta, and Toronto. What this chapter attempts to do is apply a microscope to a sub-set of the

---

[5] See, for example, the members of the Community of Practice convened at the Bellagio Center in May 2023, https://www.heinz.cmu.edu/faculty-research/profiles/mendelson-sarah/post bellagiooutcomedocumentcommunity ofpracticesddsgandhumanrights.pdf. Among the most senior foreign policy experts newly subscribed to this closer-to-home trend is Richard Haass, the former long-time head of the Council on Foreign Relations. See https://www.nytimes.com/2023/07/01/us/politics/richard-haass-biden-trump-foreign-policy.html. See also https://richardhaass.substack.com/p/announcing-home-and-away. Other examples include long-time democracy promotion organizations that, until 2020, had worked exclusively internationally such as the Carter Center standing up new efforts to apply international expertise to US elections. It should be noted that this trend has some precedent. See Larry Cox and Dorothy Q. Thomas, editors, "Close to Home: Case Studies of Human Rights Work in the United States," The Ford Foundation, June 2004, https://www.fordfoundation.org/wp-content/uploads/2015/03/2004-close_to_home.pdf.

[6] "Covid-19 Relief: States' and Localities' Fiscal Recovery Funds as of March 31, 2023," GAO-24-106753, Report to Congressional Committees, October 11, 2023, https://www.gao.gov/assets/d24106753.pdf

[7] Nancy Lindborg and Sarah Mendelson, "16 Peace, Justice and Strong Institutions," November 2020, The Brookings Institution, https://www.brookings.edu/wp-content/uploads/2020/11/16.pdf.

social justice issues we explored in the two American cities to see if a positive impact is detectable.

What we found mirrors narratives that appear almost daily in the press. At the macro level, the US economy has recovered from the pandemic.[8] As of late 2023 and early 2024, it appears, however, many American families have not. One study has found that "racial and wealth inequities have deepened since the Pandemic."[9] Moreover, as another analyst of inequality in the US has argued,

> reliance on aggregate and average numbers ... mask the nature of the economy Americans experience. Focusing on G.D.P. is a mistake, as it obscures the range of financial success and hardship in an economy as unequal as that of the United States.[10]

Put yet another way, as the Nobel Prize winning economist Angus Deaton has noted, "capitalism in America today is not working for two-thirds of adults who do not have a B.A."[11]

Writing prior to the pandemic, the situation in many predominately Black communities was especially dire, according to the

---

[8] Goldman Sachs, "The Global Economy Will Perform Better than Many Expect in 2024," November 10, 2023, https://www.goldmansachs.com/intelligence/pages/the-global-economy-will-perform-better-than-many-expect-in-2024.html.

[9] Rajashri Chakrabarti, Natalia Emanuel, and Ben Lahey, "Racial and Ethnic Wealth Inequality in the Post-Pandemic Era," *Liberty Street Economics*, February 7, 2024, Racial and Ethnic Wealth Inequality in the Post-Pandemic Era - Liberty Street Economics (newyorkfed.org) as cited in Hutchins Center Roundup, The Brookings Institution, February 8, 2024. See also the Monmouth University Poll in which few Americans "see direct benefits" from the economy, February 20, 2024, https://www.monmouth.edu/polling-institute/reports/monmouthpoll_us_022024/.

[10] Karen Petrou, "Why Bidenomics has a mortal enemy, and it isn't Trump," *New York Times*, November 16, 2023, https://www.nytimes.com/2023/11/16/opinion/why-voters-arent-buying-bidens-boasts-about-bidenomics.html.

[11] Angus Deaton, "What's the Matter with Capitalism?" *Nexus Lecture*, Amsterdam, December 17, 2022, 12, https://deaton.scholar.princeton.edu/sites/g/files/toruqf3726/files/documents/Nexus%20Lecture%20with%20figures%20%28002%29.pdf.

physician and social epidemiologist David A. Ansell. He argued that people living in those neighborhoods "...have life expectancies closer to those in developing countries...."[12] He observed that "the gap between the US county with the highest life expectancy and the one with the lowest life expectancy is between thirty and thirty five years, more than twice the gap between Haiti and the United States."[13] He went on to observe that "Black America lags thirty places behind the United States as a whole on the Human Development Index....If Black America were a country, we would have to send in foreign aid."[14]

That was the context prior to the pandemic. Since much of the government's pandemic relief efforts ended, have yet to be allocated, or do not cover the issues that American families were and are facing, numerous articles have reported the overall lack of a just recovery.[15] New York City has been especially hard hit: "the poverty rate has soared to 23 percent."[16] While child poverty in the United States was halved briefly in 2021, once the tax relief ended, by 2022, it had more than doubled to 12.4%.[17] Infant mortality

---

[12] Ansell, *The Death Gap*, xxii.

[13] Ansell, *The Death Gap*, 22.

[14] Ansell, *The Death Gap*, 41. For a similar argument focused on Americans living in poverty compared to those living in countries where USAID sends foreign assistance, see Matthew Desmond, *Poverty, By America* (New York, 2023), especially page 18.

[15] "Covid-19 Relief," (GAO). See, for example, on funding not spent in Pittsburgh, Charlie Wolfson, "Pittsburgh Has Spent Just a Quarter of Its Federal Covid Relief as Neighborhoods Await Improvements," *Public Source*, August 16, 2022, https://www.publicsource.org/pittsburgh-arpa-relief-money-gainey-land-bank-infrastructure-allegheny-county/. Nocera and McLean report of the initial funds from the CARES Act, which included $175 billion for hospitals, the most money went to "big and prosperous hospitals" rather than where the needs were greatest because the "payout formula was essentially based on past revenues," 94–95.

[16] Reporting on 2022 levels in Stefanos Chen, "Poverty has Soared in New York, with Children Bearing the Brunt," *New York Times*, February 21, 2024; Emma G. Fitzsimons and Jeffrey C. Mays, "Is New York City Back? Not for Everyone," *New York Times*, March 5, 2024.

[17] Emily A. Shrider and John Creamer, "Poverty in the United States: 2022," September 2022, U.S. Census Bureau, https://www.census.gov/content/dam/Census/library/publications/2023/demo/p60-280.pdf Congressional

in 2023 was the worst it has been in 20 years.[18] Maternal mortality rates in the US spiked in 2021, and for Black women, they were almost at the level of the global goal (SDG 3.1) of 70 per 100,000 live births. Life expectancy rates plunged. Over 17% of American households with children were food insecure in 2022. Equally shocking, some 34 million Americans experienced some form of food insecurity.[19] Eviction rates are on the rise as is homelessness, and there are record numbers of renters who experience cost burdens where 30%–50% of their income goes to housing and utilities.[20]

From our study, the first top-line finding is that the federal funds were not only difficult to track, but they were not necessarily aligned with the specific social justice gaps that many citizens in these cities were experiencing.[21] With help from the US Government Accountability Office (GAO), I was able to find what the US Treasury and the GAO have tracked. But as GAO experts noted, the data are difficult to analyze "without local context" well beyond the scope of this study.[22] The Brookings Institution has tracked ARPA funds. What the tracker shows for Alleghany County, however, is

---

efforts are ongoing to re-introduce a more modest tax relief. https://www.brookings.edu/articles/the-new-child-tax-credit-deal-is-really-a-safety-net-deal-and-by-that-measure-it-is-only-a-start/.

[18] Roni Caryn Rabin, "Infant Deaths Have Risen for the First Time in 20 Years," *New York Times*, November 1, 2023, https://www.nytimes.com/2023/11/01/health/infant-mortality-rate-rise.html.

[19] Sarah E. Mendelson, "The US is leaving millions behind: American exceptionalism needs to change by 2030," The Brookings Institution, April 10, 2023, https://www.brookings.edu/articles/the-us-is-leaving-millions-behind-american-exceptionalism-needs-to-change-by-2030/. See also https://www.ers.usda.gov/topics/food-nutrition-assistance/food-security-in-the-u-s/key-statistics-graphics/#children and Household Food Security in the United States in 2022 (usda.gov).

[20] Joint Center for Housing Studies of Harvard, "America's Rental Housing," February 2024, 2–4, https://www.jchs.harvard.edu/sites/default/files/reports/files/Harvard_JCHS_Americas_Rental_Housing_2024.pdf.

[21] Covid Relief Funding Break Down, by the CMU students, on file with the author.

[22] "Covid-19 Relief," (GAO), and author's call with GAO expert, November 16, 2023. See also Nocera and McLean, *The Big Fail*, esp. 169–176.

that the vast majority of funds (as of June 2024) went to "government operations" (nearly 46%) and "infrastructure" (nearly 20%). In Atlanta, while only 29% went to "government operations" and zero went to infrastructure, and while the tracker notes just over $1.5 million went to address food insecurity, families, as described below, still experienced a jump in food insecurity.[23] Below, I detail briefly data on food insecurity, unemployment, and maternal mortality. The findings about these three issues only underscore the universality of the challenges to just recovery and the need for the SDGs to apply everywhere, including in high-income countries.

Second, data accessibility and disaggregated data on social justice needs varied widely across localities with most cities having little or no crucial data points by race and gender. Data lags were years long. Timely data disaggregation is, however, a key tool to identify and address gender, racial, and other inequities as well as strengthen localization. It will be impossible to deliver on the SDG principle to "Leave No One Behind" (LNOB) in both the global north as well as the global south without such data. The lack of data is in and of itself a human rights issue. The gathering and management of data also emerged as pressing issues to be addressed. In most cases, the data are compiled by national and local NGOs or emerge from other ad hoc arrangements (often with universities) and not the city government where policymaking, including most critically, budgeting takes place.

Third, this chapter reflects lessons learned from an experiential learning exercise with Carnegie Mellon students and builds on discussions that began in Room 16 in 2020 and continued at the Bellagio Center in 2023 with a focus on reframing human rights using the SDGs including the need to measure and meet the socioeconomic needs of Americans. It benefits also from a growing and rich literature that has focused on the profound inequalities that exist in the United States as human rights issues discussed below. It also parallels the reframing that is coming from none other than the UN's High Commissioner for Human Rights, Volker Türk, with

---

[23] See Local Government ARPA Investment Tracker, the Brookings Institution, Local Government ARPA Investment Tracker | Brookings. The tracker does not cover the city of Pittsburgh.

his emphasis on both the SDGs and what he calls a "human rights economy."[24] Taken together, these approaches call for a paradigm shift in how we think about, research, and address human rights to fully embrace the socioeconomic ones that, if not addressed, will drive ever more inequality in the United States. To be clear, I am not making an argument for disengaging internationally. I am arguing that for the United States to lead and bolster human rights and democracy around the world, inequalities at home must be addressed. Otherwise, the United States is weakened as a global leader, and human rights as a movement suffers. The SDGs offer a frame to help solve this conundrum.

Below, I briefly draw from the literature that assesses the dramatic inequalities in America that should be framed as a human rights crisis. I then contrast the work from the CMU capstone with that of colleagues in Los Angeles discussed in Chapter 6. I briefly provide background to the study and the various methods used, as well as highlight a few top line findings. I conclude by drawing broader implications of the approach and the findings for how to research and train differently on human rights using the SDGs. The new approach is relevant both for democratic renewal at home as well as bolstering efforts to advance human rights and democracy around the world.

WHAT NUMEROUS STUDIES HAVE BEEN TELLING US ALL ALONG

Just weeks prior to the onset of the pandemic, a group of professors from the University of Pittsburgh, along with the mayor's office released a report measuring inequality in Pittsburgh by race and gender. The findings were startling to some and painfully personal

---

[24] "Vision of the Office of the United Nations High Commissioner for Human Rights for reinforcing its work in promoting and protecting economic, social and cultural rights within the context of addressing inequalities in the recovery from the COVID-19 pandemic," July 28, 2023, A/HRC/54/35, https://www.ohchr.org/en/documents/thematic-reports/ahrc5435-vision-office-united-nations-high-commissioner-human-rights.

to others.²⁵ It spawned a lot of anger especially from Black female residents who felt that the report did not provide solutions to issues that they had long known existed, such as high maternal mortality rates, but which they noted had been ignored.²⁶ That study and its findings were not in any way unique to Pittsburgh, but the data cut against the narrative often associated with the city as one of "the most livable" in the United States. In fact, for Black residents, Pittsburgh was one of the least livable cities with mortality rates higher than in 98% of similar cities.²⁷

Similarly, in 2017, a practicing physician with long experience working in both a public safety-net hospital and an academic hospital in Chicago published *The Death Gap: How Inequality Kills*. His main point had to do with the extremes in life expectancy rates in the United States between communities and argued because Americans view health as a commodity rather than as a human right, we tolerate these extreme inequalities. He offered concrete recommendations for how to lower these gaps in life expectancy including through universal health care. As the only high-income country without it, we have literally brought the life expectancy of all Americans down.²⁸

Among human rights scholars and practitioners prior to COVID, Philip Alston had long paid attention to the pervasive and persistent social justice gaps in the United States. He is also one of the few human rights experts who tracked the predecessor to the

---

²⁵ Junia Howell, Sara Goodkind, Leah Jacobs, Dominique Branson and Elizabeth Miller, "Pittsburgh's Inequality across Gender and Race," Gender Analysis White Papers, City of Pittsburgh's Gender Equity Commission, 2019, https://www.socialwork.pitt.edu/sites/default/files/pittsburghs_inequality_across_gender_and_race_07_19_20_compressed.pdf. Note that this 2019 report relied on 2016 data, then the most up-to-date data.

²⁶ Author's participation in the 2019 Allegheny Non-Profit Summit, December 3, 2019; "A Conversation on Black Livability in Pittsburgh with Rep. Lindsay Powell, Former Mayor William Peduto, and Janine Jelks-Seale," Heinz College, CMU, February 1, 2024.

²⁷ "Pittsburgh's Inequality," 23.

²⁸ Ansell, *Death Gap*. See also the yearlong *Washington Post* investigation, "Dying Early: America's Life Expectancy Crisis," October 3, 2023, https://www.washingtonpost.com/health/interactive/2023/american-life-expectancy-dropping/.

SDGs, the Millennium Development Goals (MDGs). In 2005, he reviewed rather negatively the gap between the rights community and the development community calling them "ships passing in the night."[29] Indeed, his critique that the MDGs missed the boat with regards to human rights, to carry on the metaphor, contrasts starkly with the SDGs. Reading the 2005 article nearly 20 years later, I was struck by how many MDG targets carried over to the SDGs, such as infant mortality rates and access to clean drinking water, all the while grounded in the International Covenant on Economic, Social and Cultural Rights, to which the United States is one of 71 signatories, while 171 countries are also parties to the treaty.

In 2015, as Special Rapporteur on extreme poverty and human rights, Alston turned his gaze on, among other countries, the United States and was bracing in his critique of the human rights movement. "Extreme inequality should ... be seen as a cause for shame on the part of the international human rights movement."[30] In his 2017 statement for the HRC and his final report regarding the US, he was scathing.

> *The United States is one of the world's richest, most powerful and technologically innovative countries; but neither its wealth nor its power nor its technology is being harnessed to address the situation in which 40 million people continue to live in poverty*

and called out the negative side of "American exceptionalism."[31] The persistent poverty he noted in his final report is the result of specific policy decisions including "successive administrations...determinedly

---

[29] Philip Alston, "Ships Passing in the Night: The Current State of the Human Rights and Development Debate see through the Lens of the Millennium Development Goals," *Human Rights Quarterly* 27, no. 3 (August 2005), 755–829.

[30] Philip Alston, "Extreme Inequality as the Antithesis of Human Rights," *Open Global Rights*, August 27, 2015, Extreme inequality as the antithesis of human rights | OpenGlobalRights.

[31] "Statement on Visit to the USA, by Professor Philip Alston, United States Special Rapporteur on extreme poverty and human rights," December 15, 2017, paragraphs 3, 6, and 19.

reject[ing] the idea that economic and social rights are full-fledged human rights."[32]

More recently, in 2023, sociologist Matthew Desmond also argues that persistent American poverty is designed by policies that benefit wealthier Americans as well as a result of difficulties accessing money earmarked for the poor. Echoing Ansell, he writes of how the US views health as a commodity rather than a human right. Echoing Alston, he notes the absence of a larger set of socioeconomic rights. Desmond makes the important point that it is not that some pandemic relief had no effect – specifically, the child tax credit and the moratorium on evictions – it is that they were discontinued.[33] His book is about a rich country that tolerates millions of citizens, including "one in eight children" living in poverty, with more than two million having no access to clean drinking water or flushing toilets.[34]

That rich country tolerating poverty is vividly displayed by a number of mapping projects that capture in different ways the disparities across communities in the United States. The Index of Deep Disadvantage focuses, using 2019 numbers, on several indices including poverty levels, life expectancy, and infant mortality.[35] Another effort looks at variation in distress across the United States to the neighborhood level also using a number of indicators such as employment, housing, and education. In the February 2024 edition, they find about 15.6% of the US population lives in "distressed zip codes." That translates to 51.5 million people. Another 19.2% are "at risk" including nearly 63 million people.[36] The Centers for Disease Control has its own set of indicators for social vulnerability.[37]

---

[32] "Report of the Special Rapporteur on extreme poverty and human rights on his mission to the United States of America," May 4, 2018, A/HRC/38/33/Add.1, paragraph 12.
[33] *Poverty*, 133–34.
[34] *Poverty*, 6.
[35] Understanding Communities of Deep Disadvantage (umich.edu) My thanks to Anthony Pipa for drawing my attention to various indices and trackers.
[36] 2024 DCI Interactive Map – Economic Innovation Group (eig.org) These numbers primarily derive from "the U.S. Census Bureau's American Community Survey" 2017–2021.
[37] CDC/ATSDR Social Vulnerability Index (SVI).

Cumulatively, they paint a portrait of a deeply unequal country, a distressed democracy.

Finally, beyond the literature, analysis has emerged from the Office of the High Commissioner for Human Rights laying out a "vision" about human rights to accelerate socioeconomic rights using the SDG frame specifically to address the rise in inequalities following the pandemic. "The pandemic and its aftermath vividly exposed decades of underinvestment in economic, social, and cultural rights."[38] Volker Türk's vision of a "human rights economy" is one that, if implemented, would address many of the issues detailed in the literature, laid out in this chapter, and elsewhere in this edited volume. It is a vision of an economy that puts economic, social, and cultural rights at least on par with political and civil rights and "ensure(s) better allocation of social spending in areas such as health, social security, water services, sanitation, and education."[39] It is a vision that holds out the possibility of "…operationaliz(ing) the principle of leaving no one behind…." driving a paradigm shift in how we talk about and work on human rights.[40]

LESSONS IN EXPERIENTIAL LEARNING, HUMAN RIGHTS, AND THE SDGs

If the literature and some practitioners were already moving beyond the standard human rights focus on civil and political rights and refocused on the failure to deliver on socioeconomic rights in the United States, the work has been bolstered by the adoption of the SDGs. Yet how best to engage the next generation on this agenda? Because of crosscutting aspects of the SDGs, and the complexity involved in the implementation of the SDGs, generating fluency in the framework for students, especially if only tackled as abstract concepts, is challenging.

---

[38] "Vision of the Office of the United Nations High Commissioner for Human Rights," para 15; see also para 21.
[39] "Vision of the Office of the United Nations High Commissioner for Human Rights," paras 23 and 22.
[40] "Vision of the Office of the United Nations High Commissioner for Human Rights," para 32.

Among those who have pioneered work with students on the SDGs are colleagues in Los Angeles, coming from multiple local universities, working closely with the Mayor's Office, and supported by philanthropy. Throughout our CMU effort, we consulted regularly with colleagues from the University of Southern California and on occasion with the Mayor's Office. As is evident from the description in Chapter 6, as well as other articles on their effort, the L.A. Task Forces have been doing such work in a scaled manner for several years.[41]

I will briefly compare and contrast the CMU project with the excellent work done in Los Angeles because there are lessons to be carried forward. Ours was an overly complicated project that uncovered findings, but perhaps more importantly, it also suggested new and different ways of working. Theirs is a story of iteration and scaling up. Both are examples of using the SDGs to engage students on human rights in a way that makes issues concrete rather than abstract. Our efforts validated experiential learning as an especially productive approach to help students become familiar with the SDGs through the production of knowledge in collaboration with local stakeholders – in Los Angeles, the Mayor's Office, and in the CMU work, with various local NGOs. The L.A. Task Forces focused on one, albeit complex and large, city. Our work focused on three (although we report here on two). Their work was done in deep and iterated collaboration with the Mayor's Office over several years and supported generously by philanthropy.[42] We too benefited from philanthropic support – from The Rockefeller Foundation and the Packard Foundation – albeit with smaller grants.

---

[41] Gaea Morales, Erin Bromaghim, Angela Kim, Caroline Diamond, Alejo Maggini, Avery Everhart, Sofia Gruskin, and Anthony Tirado Chase, "Classroom Walls and City Hall: Mobilizing Local Partnerships to Advance the Sustainable Development Agenda," *Sustainability* 13 (May 2021), 6173; Madeline Baer and Heidi Nichols Haddad, "Localizing the International Relations Classroom: Evaluation of Academic Partnerships with City Government," *International Studies Perspectives* 0 (2022), 1–17. On SDG pedagogy more generally, see Heidi Gibson. *From Ideas to Action: Transforming Learning to Inspire Action on Critical Global Issues* (Smithsonian Institution Scholarly Press Book, 2021), https://doi.org/10.5479/si.15173715.

[42] The Conrad Hilton Foundation spent several million dollars on local initiatives geared toward advancing the SDGs, https://www.hiltonfoundation.org/sdgs.

Between 2018 and 2020 – as a precursor to our capstone work described below and at an earlier Bellagio convening – colleagues and I had informal contact with the Mayor's Office in Pittsburgh. We made good connections with colleagues there and one of our students co-authored Pittsburgh's first Voluntary Local Review, but ultimately, we found Mayors' Offices unstable. Former Mayor Peduto, an SDG enthusiast (and now affiliated with CMU), was replaced by a mayor who has shown no interest in the SDGs, and who has apparently a mixed record advancing post-COVID recovery more generally in the city.[43] Anticipating that change in interest, our effort in 2021 pivoted to what we found to be a more promising approach and one we wish to build on; iterated engagement with local NGOs. We were guided by the social justice issues *they* flagged that they were confronting before COVID and their assessment as to whether the funds had an impact. We supplemented their answers with data where and when we could.

The L.A. effort was much larger and longer (and ongoing) involving 20 plus projects. This capstone project in contrast had a different origin story and a basic main question we were trying to answer coming out of a series of discussions in summer 2020 as part of the Brookings/Rockefeller Foundation flagship 17 rooms exercise. Ours was modest – involving work in summer 2021, the academic year 2021–2022, summer 2022, and summer 2023. Ten CMU students engaged in total versus over 160 students across Los Angeles. We had three faculty advisors at CMU and a laborious process getting IRB certified which the L.A. universities were not required to do. In Spring 2022, CMU students interviewed local stakeholders (confirming what we had heard previously – housing and food insecurity were top of mind) and attempted to find data and especially disaggregated data to understand who had been affected. The CMU students and the stakeholders along with colleagues from L.A. then went to The Hague for a workshop on the margins of the World Justice Forum confirming that the cities were

---

[43] See Wolfson "Pittsburgh Has Spent Just a Quarter of Its Federal Covid Relief as Neighborhoods Await Improvements."

not gathering disaggregated data, and the NGOs were then either trying to do it themselves or operating without any data.[44]

We initially set out to project where we would end up by 2030 on specific social justice issues. Would a city meet the SDG target or not? We tried to translate existing data into SDG targets and then project the actual numbers of people affected, building on a methodology – using "exponential smoothing" – that Brookings Institution colleagues, John W. McArthur and Krista Rasmussen, developed, as a way of taking LNOB seriously.[45] If a country uses aggregate data and reports that 97% of the population experienced food security, then who are the three percent that were food insecure? What does the percentage mean in terms of number of people? Three percent can mean millions of people, and what does that look like over time? These are all critical questions, but we ultimately did not have enough data; McArthur and Rasmussen had used Canadian data to project the numbers by province while we could not get full access to city-level data that was disaggregated. The students also found methodologically that linear regression was more manageable than exponential smoothing giving them greater parsimony and replicability.

Following IRB certification, through interviews with local stakeholders and the assessment of local data, and where possible, disaggregated data, the teams and I examined whether social justice needs, reflected in a number of goals associated with the SDG16+ agenda, were being met, where data gaps existed, and whether and how local voice had a role to play in meeting these needs and closing these gaps. Along the way, we also learned lessons about data collection and local voice that will shape follow on-work and

---

[44] Sarah Mendelson, "Heinz in the Hague," Heinz CMU Media, July 2022, https://www.heinz.cmu.edu/media/2022/July/heinz-in-the-hague

[45] John W. McArthur and Krista Rasmussen, "Who and What Gets Left Behind? Assessing Canada's Domestic Status on the Sustainable Development Goals," The Brookings Institution, October 3, 2017, https://www.brookings.edu/articles/who-and-what-gets-left-behind-assessing-canadas-domestic-status-on-the-sustainable-development-goals/, and John W McArthur and Krista Rasmussen, "Classifying Sustainable Development Goal Trajectories: A Country-level Methodology for Identifying Which Issues and People are Getting Left Behind," *World Development* 123 (November 2019), https://www.sciencedirect.com/science/article/pii/S0305750X19301846#f0005.

which became the focus of much discussion at the strategic convening in May 2023 at the Bellagio Center.[46]

FINDINGS AND COMPLEXITIES IN TWO AMERICAN CITIES AND IMPLICATIONS FOR SDG IMPLEMENTATION

Here I report just a few of the findings the teams found in Pittsburgh and Atlanta as well as supplement them. The areas of focus came after consultation with a cross section of local stakeholders, including academics and non-profit leaders. We sought (and only occasionally found) data on a range of issues including Food Support/SNAP (SDG 2.1) Maternal Mortality Rates (SDG 3.1); Infant Mortality Rates (SDG 3.2); Unemployment Rates (SDG 8.5); Shelter Visits (SDG 11.1); and Housing Cost Overburden Rates greater than 30% of income (SDG 11.1).

By drawing on the goals, targets, and indicators, or creating proxy ones, experts, citizens, and policy makers alike in theory can track progress or lack thereof. According to this approach, it is extremely likely that neither Pittsburgh nor Atlanta is on track to reach the majority of SDG targets. This situation is not unusual. In September 2023, at the midpoint to 2030, the UN reported that the world was off track with only about 15% on track.[47]

Food insecurity was flagged repeatedly by local stakeholders. Looking closely at some of the findings, the aggregate numbers do not begin to tell the complete story of who is most affected. The Charts 7.1 and 7.2 for the households in Pittsburgh and Atlanta below on the federal Supplemental Nutrition Assistance Program (SNAP), for example, when disaggregated by race, show how dramatically different the picture looks for white and Black populations.[48]

---

[46] Sarah Mendelson, Community of Practice, "Synthesis Document—Toward a Paradigm Shift: Creating a Community of Practice on Human Rights and the Sustainable Development Goals," July 20, 2023, https://www.heinz.cmu.edu/faculty-research/profiles/mendelson-sarah/postbellagiooutcomedocumentcommunityofpracticesddsgandhumanrights.pdf.
[47] https://unstats.un.org/sdgs/report/2023/progress-chart/
[48] These charts draw on the work CMU students did from 2021 to 2023 using the American Community Survey (US Census) and then were checked and finalized by former CMU and current Oxford University doctoral student Adam Koling.

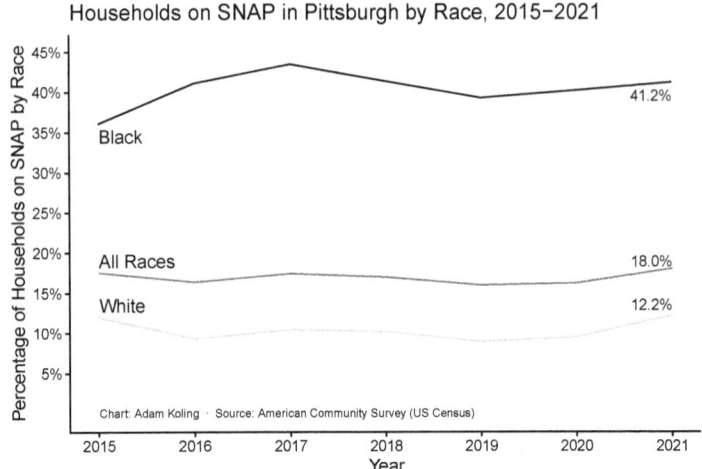

Chart 7.1. Households on SNAP in Pittsburgh by Race, 2015–2021.

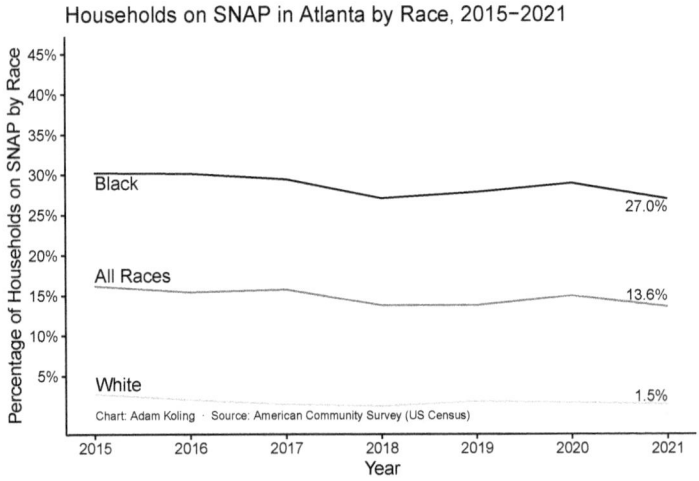

Chart 7.2. Households on SNAP in Atlanta by Race, 2015–2021.

Recent reports suggest, in fact, that in Pennsylvania, the number of SNAP recipients surged in 2023. The detailed examination suggests that people working with local communities in need witness an economy that contrasts starkly with the rosy picture senior Biden administration officials tend to paint. In early 2024, the top White House economic advisor reported, "Any way you look at it, the American economy looks upbeat."⁴⁹ Yet those working closer to the ground, quoted just days before the White House advisor's comments were issued, found

> the combination of all of the other things that are happening right now, with stagnant wages, the loss of other benefits, like the child tax credit. All of these things are kind of contributing to the struggle that people have with putting food on the table.⁵⁰

For Atlanta residents, the situation was perhaps even worse, with large delays for as many as nearly 125,000 people.⁵¹ As 2023 closed, families relying on SNAP were reporting "I can't afford to feed my family."⁵² Yet these findings emerge despite the outlay of over $1.5 million in food assistance that can be traced from ARPA funds to the city of Atlanta.⁵³

The historic data from Pittsburgh and Atlanta show that Black residents were more likely than white residents to struggle with obtaining employment by large margins. While the aggregate number in Pittsburgh in 2015 was about 7%, the disaggregated data

---

⁴⁹ Lael Brainard as quoted in Neil Irwin and Courtney Brown, "'Looks Upbeat': How the U.S. Economy Reversed a Gloomy Narrative," *Axios*, January 26, 2024, https://www.axios.com/2024/01/26/inflation-economy-interest-rates-federal-reserve?utm_source=newsletter&utm_medium=email&utm_campaign=newsletter_axiosam&stream=top.

⁵⁰ Sally Ellwein, director of meeting basic needs, United Way of Southwestern Pennsylvania, as quoted in Jordan Anderson, "Pennsylvania is seeing record SNAP participation," *Pittsburgh Post-Gazette*, January 19, 2024, https://www.post-gazette.com/news/social-services/2024/01/19/pennsylvania-snap-benefits-participation/stories/202401180124.

⁵¹ Rachel Aragon, "'It's a Struggle: Georgians report SNAP Benefits Delay as State Works to Resolve Backlog," *Atlanta News First*, November 16, 2023, https://www.atlantanewsfirst.com/2023/11/16/its-struggle-georgians-report-snap-benefits-delay-state-works-resolve-backlog/.

⁵² As reported in Rachel Aragon, "SNAP Delays Leave Georgia Families Worried about Food Delays Days before Christmas," *Atlanta News First*, December 22, 2023, https://www.atlantanewsfirst.com/2023/12/21/thousands-georgians-waiting-snap-benefits-be-approved/.

⁵³ On the city of Atlanta, see the Local Government ARPA Investment Tracker, The Brookings Institution, Local Government ARPA Investment Tracker | Brookings. The tracker does not cover the city of Pittsburgh.

show that it was around 17% for Black residents. When we look at the data for 2021, from the US Census, the story is much the same. Large gaps persist and unemployment rates for Black citizens are high at just over 15%. In Atlanta, it is similar: the chart drawing on US Census data show the number for 2015 in the aggregate at about 7% but for the Black population it is about 13%. The trends continued, although with some relief for both Black and white populations in 2021. The main takeaway, however, from the Charts 7.3 and 7.4, is that pointing to the aggregate unemployment rate in Atlanta of 5.2% or in Pittsburgh of 7.2% for 2021 obscures the true economic picture for many citizens.

In assessing maternal mortality, not only do data gaps and data lags loom large, but what emerges as especially problematic is an assessment that solely looks at the aggregate numbers. The pandemic exacerbated disparities. As two authors note as part of the overall "fail" in the American response to the pandemic, "COVID-19 didn't just shine a spotlight on the problems in our health-care system; it stacked multiple inequities on top of one another."[54] Chart 7.5 shows US mortality rates by race from 2018 to 2021 as tracked by the US Centers for Disease Control and Prevention (CDC).

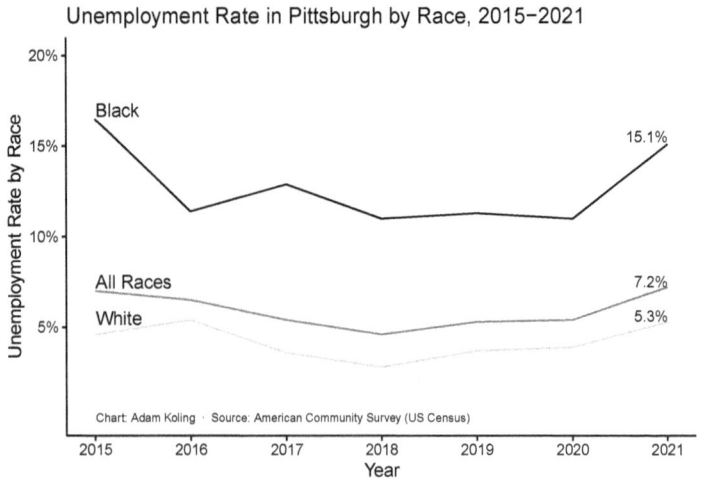

Chart 7.3. Unemployment Rate in Pittsburgh by Race, 2015–2021.

---

[54] Nocera and McLean, *The Big Fail*, 80.

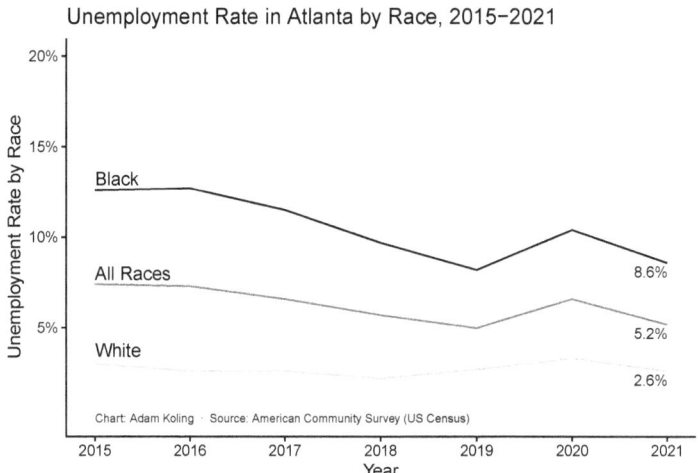

Chart 7.4. Unemployment Rate in Atlanta by Race, 2015–2021.

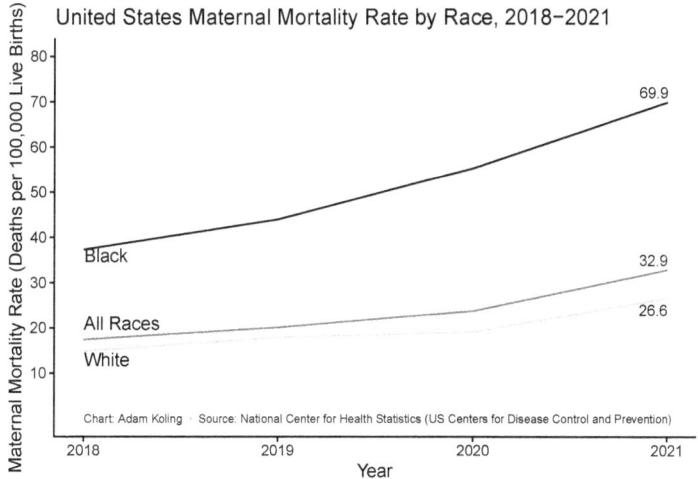

Chart 7.5. United States Maternal Mortality Rate by Race, 2018–2021.

Disaggregated data for maternal mortality rates are not publicly available in Pittsburgh or Atlanta. Data are aggregated and released only years later. The CMU students reported:

> *In the United States, state-level maternal mortality data is aggregated and distributed in reports by Maternal Mortality Review Committees (MMRCs).*

> MMRCs are multidisciplinary committees that convene at the state or local level to comprehensively review deaths that occur during or within a year of pregnancy (pregnancy-associated deaths). They include representatives from public health, obstetrics and gynecology, maternal-fetal medicine, nursing, midwifery, forensic pathology, mental and behavioral health, patient advocacy groups, and community-based organizations. There are concerns about privacy related to this data.... Therefore, the raw data that MMRCs utilize is not publicly available until it is aggregated by the respective state MMRC, and subsequently turned into a public report. Each MMRC reports their data differently, and on different timelines (i.e. Georgia aggregates their data by three-year increments making annual trend analysis impossible). This makes comparison of trends across different states difficult. Due to these complications, and the limited time and resources of the #JR [Just Recovery] team at CMU [as the capstone team referred to itself], state and provincial-level maternal mortality data was inaccessible.[55]

The CMU team noted that the

> lack of maternal mortality data is evident from the PA Department of Health's website which states that, 'There is a lot that we do not know. To better understand maternal mortality and how to prevent these deaths, Pennsylvania established the Pennsylvania Maternal Mortality Review Committee (PA MMRC) to review all pregnancy associated deaths in the commonwealth.'

The team also noted:

> Prior to the creation of the PA MMRC, there was no statewide effort in Pennsylvania to review maternal deaths. The PA MMRC report that came out in 2021 reviews the

---

[55] CMU/Heinz Students, "Maternal Mortality Data Challenges" (on file with author).

> maternal deaths in Pennsylvania during 2018. This is the most recent maternal mortality data that the PA MMRC has released.

The team that worked on this project in summer 2022

> reached out to multiple maternal and child healthcare experts from the University of Pittsburgh, Allegheny County Health Department, Carnegie Mellon University, and the MMRC members to figure out where the team could find the maternal mortality statistics for Pittsburgh. These professionals either cited unavailability of data or suggested trying sources ... which do not have the required data.[56]

Here is a sampling of comments they received from the experts: "Unfortunately, receipt of these data from the state usually lags about two years behind, lately even more so with delays from COVID and prioritization of death records," according to an official at the Allegheny County Health Department. (As if maternal mortality rates were not relevant or related to death records?) From an official at UPMC: "If there is any local data, it has not been analyzed to assess its accuracy which of course would have significant limitations." A local journalist in late October 2023 confirmed these findings.[57] In Atlanta, the story is the same: the CDC and the Department of Public Health aggregate at the state level.

Were more recent data available by race for Pittsburgh and Atlanta, as we have seen when we do have access, the findings for Black women would likely be terrible. Nationally, the CDC reported a sharp rise in 2021 in the United States when Black women

---

[56] CMU/Heinz Students, "Maternal Mortality Data Challenges" (on file with author). See also https://www.health.pa.gov/topics/healthy/Pages/Maternal-Mortality.aspx.

[57] The detailed correspondence with these experts can be found in "Maternal Mortality Data Challenges" (on file with the author). See Hanna Webster, "Black maternal mortality rates are rising," *Pittsburgh Post-Gazette*, October 27, 2023.

experienced 69.9 maternal deaths per 100,000.[58] That ratio is just below the 70 deaths per 100,000 that the World Health Organization has set *globally* for the SDG target to reduce maternal mortality by 2030.[59] The United States is last in terms of high-income countries on maternal mortality. Compare the *aggregated* maternal mortality rate for the United States in 2021: the ratio was 31 per 100,000. In comparison, the average maternal death rates in the UK and in Western Europe were 4, in Eastern Europe 12, and in Central Asia 24 per 100,000 for 2021, according to the Gates Foundation.[60]

Missing disaggregated data ultimately means it is difficult – if not impossible – to assess who is being left behind. Data gaps and data lags, especially those concerning disaggregated data by race, gender, and geographic boundary, make it impossible to issue solid predictions about the future of the SDGs in these cities. If this is the case in American cities, we assume it is true in many cities throughout the world. As the world closes in on the 2030 agenda, the need for disaggregated data, the gold standard, is urgent.

While each city has missing data needed to measure accurate progress on the SDGs, it should be noted that Pittsburgh did conduct two Voluntary Local Reviews.[61] The interviews with the stakeholders and the workshop in the Hague supplemented the missing data and helped fill in gaps. But the issue of who is responsible for collecting data in these cities emerged as a major issue. Cities may not have funds and expect the non-profits to do the collection. The non-profits do not necessarily have the data analytic skills nor the funding to do the work. In some cases, one does have to wonder if

---

[58] Donna L. Hoyert, "Maternal Mortality Rates in the United States, 2021," *CDC*, March 2023, https://www.cdc.gov/nchs/data/hestat/maternal-mortality/2021/maternal-mortality-rates-2021.htm.

[59] WHO, "SDG Target 3.1," https://www.who.int/data/gho/data/themes/topics/indicator-groups/indicator-group-details/GHO/maternal-mortality#:~:text=SDG%20Target%203.1%20%7C%20Maternal%20mortality,per%20100%20000%20live%20births.

[60] "Global Progress and Projections for Maternal Mortality," *The Gates Foundation*, 2022, https://www.gatesfoundation.org/goalkeepers/report/2022-report/progress-indicators/maternal-mortality/.

[61] See https://engage.pittsburghpa.gov/pgh-VLR.

there is a political reason for not collecting and therefore measuring progress. A future research question for the Community of Practice referenced in the introduction to this edited volume, in assessing the hundreds of Voluntary Local Reviews (VLRs) that have been generated since 2016, is: do the VLRs access disaggregated data or instead opt for a mainly qualitative story? As Oxford University professor Daniel Armanios commented in Bellagio in May 2023, the politics of measurement need to be considered in cities. "What is being measured? Who is being asked?"[62] A more general question going forward, noted by Columbia University professor Jack Snyder also in Bellagio, "how might we make the need for data gathering politically persuasive to policy makers?"[63]

THE SDGs, THE HUMAN RIGHTS ECONOMY, AND THE PARADIGM SHIFT

Experiential learning and capstone projects based on systems thinking are ideal modalities for engaging students on the SDGs. The approach in the CMU project was, however, overly complicated and burdened – turn over in student groups, three cities, IRB certification delays, data gaps, and multiple SDGs. That said, the study uncovered several critical findings. First, that the focus on LNOB is an important principle to add to the human rights pedagogy, and second, that the elevation of socioeconomic rights is critical in the United States today. Third, fundamentally, we need a better way to get timely disaggregated data, and we need to figure out how to build an open-source data portal that can show what is going on in real time. This will no doubt involve establishing close links to local stakeholders in a way that benefits them and in which they are engaged in the creation of data. We then need to translate the findings for policy makers (as colleagues did in Los Angeles) to generate policy responses. As the OHCHR vision notes, "the lack of updated, quality and

---

[62] Author's notes, Bellagio Convening, May 2023.
[63] Author's notes, Bellagio Convening, May 2023. See also Jack Snyder, *Human Rights for Pragmatists: Social Power in Modern Times* (Princeton University Press, 2022).

disaggregated data obscures inequalities and stands in the way of fulfilling the commitment to leave no one behind."[64]

As we arrive at the midpoint to 2030, there are a lot of calls for "rescuing" the SDGs and also, perhaps more helpfully, for "doing things differently."[65] I conclude by offering an approach that arose from this study; we need a paradigm shift in how we teach, train, and research on human rights that applies to human rights work at home and around the world. It also derives from my experience as the lead at USAID from 2010 to 2014 on democracy, human rights, and governance. On many occasions, I experienced what Alston described as "ships passing in the night." Sometimes, it was more like ships crashing in the night. Rights were viewed as separate and apart, and even at odds, from development by many colleagues. The SDG framework when implemented can help lessen those dynamics, but we need a workforce fluent in the SDGs. Innovations in higher education offer pathways to help create such fluency. Specifically, universities have a critical role to play in generating a refreshed approach to human rights that includes SDG literacy, helping grow "Cohort 2030," all in collaboration with cities and local communities. [66]

What would such a paradigm shift look like? It has four interrelated elements:

Elevate socioeconomic rights;

Localize global norms and translate them into local action;

Generate disaggregated data that can inform policy recommendations; and

Scale the community of practice dedicated to these issues.

---

[64] "OHCHR Vision," para 49.

[65] "The SDGs Second Half," Center for Sustainable Development, The Brookings Institution, April 5, 2023, https://www.brookings.edu/articles/the-sdgs-second-half-ideas-for-doing-things-differently/.

[66] Sarah Mendelson, "Young People, the Sustainable Development Goals, and the Liberal World Order: What is to be done?" *Medium*, October 9, 2018, https://medium.com/sdg16plus/young-people-the-sustainable-development-goals-and-the-liberal-world-order-what-is-to-be-done-fc648e3b2d21.

The SDG principle to leave no one behind needs to be embedded in human rights education. LNOB is fundamentally a call for human rights to be respected universally; the SDGs apply everywhere to everyone. The SDGs help broaden attention beyond political and civil rights and elevate socioeconomic ones, which during the Cold War, became enmeshed in East-West power struggles and were subsequently downplayed, at least in the United States.[67] The pandemic laid bare the urgent need to address social justice and socioeconomic inequities in the global north as well as in the global south. These issues are bound up with what imperils democracy in the United States.

Human rights education should also focus on SDG localization and translation in specific contexts (sometimes referred to as "vernacularization" in the rights literature).[68] Some human rights scholars have noted that it is the very lack of localization that has created significant barriers to the realization of rights.[69] When viewed as only global and abstract rather than local and experienced by people, the disconnect drives or contributes to the current end-times-for-human-rights *zeitgeist*. Localizing the SDGs, as has occurred in cities around the world, and gauged through VLRs, has resulted in innovation and practical applications that directly and positively impact communities.[70] These efforts at localization are worthy of study for good practices and examples of success.

Closely related to both LNOB and localization, human rights and sustainable development research and coursework should

---

[67] Sarah Mendelson, "Inequality, the SDGs, and the human rights movement in the United States and around the world," *The Brookings Institution*, June 12, 2020, https://www.brookings.edu/articles/inequality-the-sdgs-and-the-human-rights-movement-in-the-us-and-around-the-world/.

[68] Sally Engle Merry and Peggy Levitt, "The Vernacularization of Women's Human Rights," in *Human Rights Futures* eds. Stephen Hopgood, Jack Snyder and Leslie Vinjamuri (Cambridge University Press, 2017), https://www.cambridge.org/core/books/abs/human-rights-futures/vernacularization-of-womens-human-rights/427B9B2BA774942F5F1E5A6B2119091B.

[69] Merry and Levitt, "The Vernacularization of Women's Human Rights."

[70] UN Habitat keeps a running list of the Voluntary Local Reviews, https://unhabitat.org/topics/voluntary-local-reviews.

increasingly incorporate and/or generate people-centered data ecosystems. There are a number of ways to do this including through building community data portals using open-source software with the input of local community members. Ideally, this would be an iterative process, drawing on artificial intelligence platforms. As discussed during the 2021 flagship 17 Rooms exercise and validated during the 2022 Hague workshop, there is a growing demand among rights and social justice experts for the creation of such data ecosystems. Disaggregated data concerning local communities' social justice gaps are necessary (along with policies and funds) to enable more just transitions post-pandemic. The research in Pittsburgh and Atlanta revealed numerous data gaps and lags obscuring the suffering of citizens made worse by the tendency to rely on aggregated data. Then there is the added step needed to translate data in real time into policy recommendations and engage policy makers at various local, state, and federal levels to generate timely responses.

Finally, to drive this paradigm shift, we need to scale the community of practice to share lessons learned, good practices in how to engage the next generation – Cohort 2030 – on these issues, having LNOB as a watchword, focused on socioeconomic rights, using disaggregated data, engaging the communities most affected.

These four steps link the UDHR with the SDGs, in addition to the numerous subsequent treaties and laws which students still need to learn. Best of all, these could drive demand for progress on all the people-focused SDGs. The second half of the SDG era needs to create sustainable futures in which rights are realized for all – in the United States and around the world. Perhaps readers will find the recommendations in this chapter, and other chapters in this volume, cogent ways to create such futures.

ACKNOWLEDGMENTS

Many thanks to the students who worked on the project: Nicole Annunziata, Kristen Hochreiter, Jonathan Reisher, Zoe Swarzenski, Samuel Blurton, Campbell North, Ibrahim Ameer, Tiantian Zhu,

Unjust Recovery and the Need to Reframe Human Rights Using SDGs

and Andrew Nunn, as well as the faculty members who helped guide the students on data analyses, Professor Corey Harper and Professor Daniel Armanios. A special note of thanks to Daniel and his Oxford University (and former CMU) student Adam Koling for the extra assist on the charts. A Heinz College capstone project and summer research also included a case study of Toronto. For analytical reasons and space constraints, in this chapter, I report only some of the findings from just the two American cities, Pittsburgh and Atlanta. Numerous documents from the capstone and summer research work are housed with the author and available upon request. The author is also grateful to The Rockefeller Foundation and the David and Lucille Packard Foundation for support of the work detailed in this chapter.

ABOUT THE EDITOR

Sarah E. Mendelson is a Distinguished Service Professor of Public Policy at Carnegie Mellon's Heinz College, and since September 2024, leading an initiative seeking to create a Center for Sustainable Futures at CMU. She joined CMU in 2018 as the Head of CMU's Heinz College in Washington DC, a position she held until August 2024. She is also a nonresident Senior Fellow with the Center for Sustainable Development in the Global Economy and Development program at the Brookings Institution and a board member of the Free Russia Foundation. From 2015 to 2017, she served as the US Representative to the UN's ECOSOC and the Alternate US Representative to the UN General Assembly. At the US Mission to the UN, she led on international development, human rights, human trafficking, and humanitarian affairs. Prior to her appointment, she served as a Deputy Assistant Administrator at USAID in the Bureau for Democracy, Conflict, and Humanitarian Assistance from 2010 to 2014, where she was the Agency lead on democracy, human rights, and governance. Ambassador Mendelson received her BA in History from Yale University and her Ph.D. in Political Science from Columbia University.

ABOUT THE CONTRIBUTORS

Elizabeth Andersen is Executive Director of the World Justice Project, advancing the rule of law through research, advocacy, and support for a global stakeholder network. Ms Andersen has over 25 years of experience in the international legal arena, having served previously as Director of the American Bar Association Rule of Law Initiative; Executive Director of the American Society of International Law; and Executive Director of the Europe and Central Asia Division of Human Rights Watch. A member of the Council on Foreign Relations and the American Law Institute, she is the chair-elect of the Williams College Board of Trustees and serves on the governing and advisory boards of several other non-profit organizations. Ms Andersen has received a number of awards for her work in the international rule of law field, including the ABA Section of International Law World Order Under Law Award. She has a B.A. from Williams College, an M.P.A. from Princeton University, and a J.D. from Yale University.

Michelle E. Anderson's scholarship focuses on the intersection of law and policy, human rights, and inequities. Her current work centers on global health, including sexual and reproductive health, social determinants of health, and access to health services. Michelle's professional experience spans the United States, Northern Ireland, the Palestinian territories, and several African countries, particularly South Africa, where she has researched and consulted on political conflict, post-conflict recovery, and access to justice. She received her PhD from the University of Cape Town for her thesis on conflict actors, media, and transitional justice. Michelle also holds an M.Phil. in Conflict Resolution and Reconciliation from Trinity College Dublin and Undergraduate degrees in Human Rights and Anthropology from Southern Methodist University.

Ariel C. Armony serves as Provost and Executive Vice President at Babson College. From 2015 to 2024, he led the University of Pittsburgh's global engagement and strategy as the Vice Chancellor for Global Affairs and Director of the University Center for International Studies, home to seven academic centers. Prior to joining Pitt, he led the Miami Institute for Advanced Study of the Americas at the University of Miami. A political scientist, Armony has received fellowships from the Woodrow Wilson Center for Scholars and Fulbright, Rockefeller, and Kellogg Foundations. His most recent book, *Emerging Global Cities: Origin, Structure, and Significance*, explores the transformation of Dubai, Miami, and Singapore into global centers of commerce, finance, and art. He has also written extensively on the relationship between China and Latin America, democratization, and civil society.

Anthony Tirado Chase is a Professor of Diplomacy and World Affairs at Occidental College. Chase has published widely on human rights in the Middle East and globally, with a particular focus on how global norms – from human rights, the Sustainable Development Goals, and transitional justice – can be re-imagined at local levels. These themes inform his most recent book, the co-edited *Human Rights at the Intersections: Transformation Through Local, Global, and Transnational Challenges* (Bloomsbury, 2023).

Sofia Gruskin directs the USC Institute on Inequalities in Global Health (IIGH). She is a Distinguished Professor of *Population and Public Health Sciences and Law*, Professor of Preventive Medicine and Chief of the Disease Prevention, Policy and Global Health Division at the Keck School of Medicine; Professor of Law and Preventive Medicine at the Gould School of Law. Gruskin currently sits on numerous international boards and committees, including the PEPFAR Scientific Advisory Board; the *Lancet* Commission on Gender and Global Health; the IUSSP Scientific Panel on Population Registers, Ethics and Human Rights; and the *Lancet* Commission on Health and Human Rights.

Alvaro Herrero is an expert in governance, transparency, and the rule of law with extensive experience in Latin America and the Caribbean. As Undersecretary for Strategic Management and Institutional Quality in the Government of the City of Buenos Aires, he was responsible for the implementation of the 2030 Agenda, and in 2019 he led Buenos Aires to become one of the first cities in the world to submit a voluntary local review to the United Nations. He has a long history of involvement in civil rights and public policy NGOs. He is currently the Executive Director of the International Open Justice Network. His latest book, *Disruptive Cities*, is a collection of experiences from cities using the 2030 Agenda as a strategy to address the COVID-19 pandemic. He holds a law degree (Universidad Nacional de La Plata), an M.A. in Latin American Studies (Georgetown University), and a Ph.D. in Political Science (University of Oxford).

Gaea Morales is a PhD candidate in Political Science and International Relations at the University of Southern California. Her research agenda is centered on the questions of how global governance ideas translate into local action and the role of sub-national actors in shaping global politics. Her work focuses on issues and threats that transcend territorial boundaries, such as the political economy of climate change and the environment and transnational human rights movements, with regional expertise on Southeast Asian metropolitans (Metro Manila, Philippines; Bangkok, Thailand, and Jakarta, Indonesia). Her work has been published in the *Journal of Human Rights, Journal of Conflict Resolution*, and *Sustainability*. Prior to USC, she worked as a program coordinator to support the Los Angeles Mayor's Office of International Affairs' efforts to localize the Sustainable Development Goals. She graduated with a BA in Diplomacy and World Affairs and French Studies from Occidental College.

Thomas Probert is a Senior Researcher at the Centre for Human Rights (University of Pretoria), where he leads a multidisciplinary initiative aimed at bringing together the developmental fields of crime and violence prevention with the human rights-based approach toward the protection of the right to life. This has involved a close engagement with SDG 16, including serving as a consultant to the South African government in the development of its first national SDG Report in 2019. More recently he has been focusing on questions of civic freedoms, and particularly the right of peaceful assembly, first in close partnership with the UN Human Rights Committee in the development of its General Comment No.37 and has co-edited the *Oxford Handbook* on the subject. Prior to these roles, he was a research consultant and special advisor to the mandate of the UN Special Rapporteur on extrajudicial, summary, or arbitrary executions, based in the Office of the High Commissioner for Human Rights in Geneva. Thomas is also a Research Associate at the Centre of Governance and Human Rights (University of Cambridge), where he leads a research theme on justice and accountability.

INDEX

Note: Page numbers followed by *n* indicate notes.

Access to justice, 14, 47, 59, 64
  data, innovation, and
      collaboration, 15–25
  higher education, 25–35
  programs, 41
"Access to justice for all", 25,
      35, 100
Accountability, 63, 76, 100, 111
  lack of accountability culture,
      52–53
Advocacy skills of law students, 65
African Moot, 64–65
2030 Agenda, 38–39, 43, 47,
      80–81
American Bar Foundation's Justice
      Data Observatory
      initiative, 34
American Civil Liberties Union of
      Michigan, 28
American exceptionalism,
      116–123, 125
American poverty, 126
American Rescue Plan Act (ARPA),
      118, 133
Anti-corruption offices, 41
Applied research, 31, 74
Artificial intelligence, 29, 52, 142
Atlanta, 116, 118, 122, 131,
      133–135, 137, 142–143
Authoritarian forces, 5

Big data, 29, 33
Black communities, 119–120
Branding, 63, 69
Brazilian judiciary, 44
Brookings Institution, 9, 118, 121

Capitalism, 119
Carnegie Mellon University, 82, 137
Center of Law and Technology at
      Duke University Law
      School, 31, 33–34
Centers for Disease Control and
      Prevention (CDC),
      134, 137
Central American and Caribbean
      Judicial Council, 47, 56
CHANGE Network, 106, 111
Cities, 38, 121, 124, 129, 131–139
Citizen participation, 41, 53–55, 59
City government officials, 106, 112
City-academic partnerships,
      102–104
Civil society, 5, 7, 42, 53, 57, 91
Closing space phenomenon, 5–6
Cohort 2030, 3, 63, 76, 140, 142
Cold War, 4, 141
Collaboration, 15–25
  with cultural, social,
      education, or health
      institutions, 31
Colleges, 15, 26
Community of Practice, 8, 11, 87,
      116, 139
Conrad Hilton Foundation,
      128*n*42
Costa Rica judiciary, 43–44
Court-sanctioned online tools, 22
COVID-19 pandemic, 7, 22, 25
Credibility in US foreign policy,
      6, 49
Cross-sectoral collaboration,
      23–25, 31

Index

d.school, 31
Data, 7, 15–25, 71, 108–111
  gaps, 18–19, 93, 134, 138–139, 142
  governance mechanisms, 52
  lags, 93, 134, 138, 142
Data science, university strengths in, 26–32
Death Gap: How Inequality Kills, The, 124
Democracy delivering, 5, 115–116
"Developing" countries, 3, 120
Disaggregation, 72, 122
Domestic violence, 24
Domestication, 71–72, 75

Economic development, 91, 99
Education, 18, 21, 39, 48
Educational innovation, 33
Effective communications strategies, 31
Electoral Tribunal of the Federal Judiciary, 44–45
Environment, 33, 39, 60
Equality, 111
Ethical engagement, 87
Evidence-based decision-making culture, lack of, 51–52
Executive Branch agencies, 41, 48–50
Exercise, 76–77
Experiential learning, 64, 115, 122, 139
  lessons in, 127–131
  models, 115
  exercise, 122
Expertise and insights of scholars, 29
Exponential smoothing, 130

Family justice, 24
Food insecurity, 121–122, 131
Formal justice institutions, 21–22

Gender, 7, 39, 59, 93, 106
Georgetown University Law Center's Institute for Technology Law and Policy, 31

Global community, 2
Global justice gap, 16–17, 36
Global south, 3, 65, 93
Government Accountability Office (GAO), 16, 121

Hague Institute for Innovation of Law, 24–25
Health, 5, 18, 31, 33, 39, 95, 127
High Level Political Forum (HLPF), 55n26
Higher education, 9–10, 25, 85–86
  innovations in, 3, 140
  institutions of, 13
  lessons learned and recommendations, 32–35
  SDG 17, 83
  university strengths in data science, innovation, and multidisciplinary collaboration, 26–32
Higher Education Institutions (HEI), 26–27, 39, 81, 84
Housing advocate, 28
Human rights, 5, 9, 34, 39, 54, 60, 62, 80, 86–87
  data and building capacity for, 108–111
  economy, 123, 127, 139–142
  guiding principle for new human rights agenda, 86–88
  lessons in, 127–131
  at local level, 98–102
  opportunity for, 35–36
  moots, 64
  politics, 67
  practitioners, 64
  shadow reports, 64
Human Rights Council, 80
Human rights education, 62, 75
  examples from, 64–69
  potential, 75–77
Human Rights Movement, 35–36
Human Rights Promotion, 105–108

Index

Ibero-American Judicial Summit of Supreme Courts, 46–47
Index of Deep Disadvantage, 126
Indigenous mediators, 21
Indivisibility, 111
Inequality, 2, 59–60, 110, 119, 125
Inequities, 4, 11, 119, 122, 134, 141
Innovation, 15–25
  in justice services, 19–22
  university strengths in, 26–32
Instagram, 58
Institutional culture, 53
Inter-American Court of Human Rights, 58
International Covenant on Economic, Social and Cultural Rights (ICESCR), 100
International Development Law Organization, 17
International nongovernmental organizations, 57–58
International Open Justice Network, 53
International organizations, 17, 46, 56, 69

Judicial Council of Central America and the Caribbean, 46
Judicial institutions, 38–39, 47, 50, 54–59
Judiciaries, 10, 38–43, 46–47
  state of the art, 43–48
  Strategic Institutional Plan, 44
Jurisdictions, 16, 19, 22, 25
Just recovery, 9, 118, 122
JustFix.org, 22
Justice, 2, 8, 14–15, 18, 39
  data ecosystem, 15, 18–19
  gaps, 88
  problems, 20
  sector institutions, 39, 41, 54
Justice Action Coalition, 17
Justice Index, 27
Justice services, 10, 14, 20, 26, 32
  required innovation in, 19–22

Latin America and the Caribbean, 41
Law and social science schools, 39
Law schools, 16, 33, 54
Leadership in higher education, 15
Leave No One Behind (LNOB) principle, 2, 7, 14, 68, 122, 141
Legal Aid Interagency Roundtable, 25
Legal frameworks, 4–5, 8
Legal needs, 19, 27, 57
Localization, 46, 71, 101–102, 112, 141
Los Angeles, 101, 107, 123, 128
  city-academic partnerships, 103–104
  data and building capacity for human rights, 108–111
  efforts, 102–103
  and SDGs, 102–111
  TFs and Human Rights Promotion, 105–108
Los Angeles Sustainable Development Goals (L.A. SDGs), 98

Major Groups and other Stakeholders (MGoS), 99
Maternal mortality ratio, 109–110
Maternal Mortality Review Committees (MMRCs), 135
Mayor's Office of International Affairs (MOIA), 103
Millennium Development Goals (MDGs), 99, 125
Ministries of justice, 19, 41
Ministries of public security, 41
Moots, 65
Mortality, 109, 124
Multi-disciplinary centers of innovation and excellence, 15
"Multi-door courthouse" model, 24
Multi-sectoral collaboration, 25, 36
Multidisciplinary collaboration, 29
  university strengths in, 26–32
Multidisciplinary initiatives, 30

National Center for Access to Justice, 27
National Endowment for the Arts, 31–32
National nongovernmental organizations, 57–58
National Pact, 43
National Schools Moot, 66
Nondiscrimination, 111
Nongovernmental organizations (NGOs), 5–6, 57

Occidental College, 104, 106, 111
Ombudsmen, 38
Open Government Partnership, 53, 55
Open justice, 53, 55
Organization for Economic Cooperation and Development, 17
Outdated educational paradigms, 54

Packard Foundation, 128, 143
Pandemic relief, 120, 126
Paradigm shift, 3, 139–142
Participation, 48, 111
Partnerships, 31, 55–56, 58, 63, 82
Pennsylvania Maternal Mortality Review Committee (PA MMRC), 136
People-centered approach, 14, 16–17, 25
People-centered justice, 17, 19, 31
Perceptions of judicial authorities, 48
Periodic meetings, 50
Pittsburgh, 116, 118, 124, 129, 131, 133, 138, 142–143
Placing positivism in context, 67–68
Policy, 73–74
Policy makers, 18, 31–32, 139
Pomona College, 106
Post-Cold War triumphalist period, 4
Poverty, 39, 120, 126
Poverty Solutions, 28–29
Problem-solving, 21, 25, 36

Project management capacity, 50–51
Prosecutor Transparency Project, 28
Provinces, 38
Public health matters, 107
Public trust, 79, 85
Publication of information on project implementation, 50

Quantitative Study of Inclusion, Diversity, and Equity (QSIDE), 28
Quattrone Center for the Fair Administration of Justice at University of Pennsylvania Law School, 34

Race, 7, 93, 106–107, 111, 137–138
Rankings, 88, 90
Reciprocity, 87
Report drafting committees, 75
Rockefeller Foundation, 128
Rockefeller Foundation's Bellagio Center, 7
Role-play, 66, 74–75
17 Rooms, 9, 118, 129, 142
Rule of Law Policy, 17
Russia, 5–6

Shadow reporting, 67–68
Shadow reports, 68–69
 drafting process, 69–75
Simulacre SDG report drafting process, 69–75
Social justice, 7, 9, 84, 88, 95
Social networking, 58–59
Social responsibility, 87
Social worker, 28
Socioeconomic rights, 93, 116, 126–127, 139, 142
Stakeholder engagement, 112–113
Stanford Law School, 31
Stanford Legal Design Lab, 31
Subnational governments, 38
Substance abuse, 24
Summit for Democracy (2023), 17

Index

Supplemental Nutrition Assistance Program (SNAP), 131, 133
Supranational level, 56–57
Supreme Audit Institutions, 38
Supreme Court of the Dominican Republic, 45
Sustainability practices, 91–92
Sustainable Development Goals (SDGs), 2, 11, 34, 38–43, 54–59, 62, 80, 116, 139–142
  adoption, 7
  findings and complexities in American cities and implications, 131–138
  guiding principle for new human rights agenda, 86–88
  lessons in, 127–131
  at local level, 98–102
  Los Angeles and, 102–111
  marketing tool, 88–91
  moot, 66
  overcoming difficulties and challenges, 48–54
  purpose of, 4
  SDG 16+, 8, 10, 62
  SDG16, 14, 40, 42, 47, 81
Sustainable Development Goals Report (SDGR), 70–71, 74

Task Forces (TFs), 10–11, 103–108, 128
Technological innovation, 22, 31
Technology, 22, 31
Times Higher Education Impact Ranking (THE-IR), 89–91
Transparency, 41, 53, 89
Truth-in-Los Angeles project, 108

United Nations (UN), 3, 80
  agencies, 46
United Nations Development Program (UNDP), 17, 42, 56–57
United States, 4–6, 85, 103, 117, 120, 126, 138
Universal Declaration of Human Rights (UDHR), 2, 4, 116
Universality, 2, 111, 122
Universities, 10, 15, 26, 56, 81–86, 140
  data collection and analysis initiatives, 30
  partners, 106
  strengths in data science, innovation, and multidisciplinary collaboration, 26–32
Urban development, 39

Vernacularization, 141
Voluntary Local Reviews (VLRs), 49, 70, 98, 139
Voluntary National Reviews (VNRs), 49, 70
Voluntary University Review (VUR), 82–83

Web-scraping approaches, 29
"Wicked Problems" practicum, 105, 107, 109
World Bank, 17, 115, 117
World Justice Forum, 129–130
World Justice Project (WJP), 16, 23, 57–58
  Atlas of Legal Needs Surveys, 27

X, 58

YouTube, 58

www.ingramcontent.com/pod-product-compliance
Lightning Source LLC
Chambersburg PA
CBHW061941220426
43662CB00012B/1990